Transforming Foreign Aid

United States Assistance in the 21st Century

Transforming Foreign Aid

United States Assistance in the 21st Century

Carol Lancaster

INSTITUTE FOR INTERNATIONAL ECONOMICS
WASHINGTON, DC
AUGUST 2000

Carol Lancaster, visiting fellow (1987-91, 1996-98), is associate professor and director of the Master of Science in Foreign Service program at Georgetown University. She served as deputy administrator of USAID (1993-96), deputy assistant secretary of state for African affairs (1980-81), and in a number of other government positions. Her most recent book is *Aid to Africa* (University of Chicago, 1999). She has published several books with the Institute including *African Economic Reform: The External Dimension* (1991).

INSTITUTE FOR INTERNATIONAL ECONOMICS
11 Dupont Circle, NW
Washington, DC 20036-1207
(202) 328-9000   FAX: (202) 328-5432
http://www.iie.com

C. Fred Bergsten, *Director*
Brigitte Coulton, *Director of Publications and Web Development*
Brett Kitchen, *Marketing Director*

Typesetting by Sandra F. Watts
Printing by Kirby Lithographic Company, Inc.
Cover design by Naylor Design Inc.

Printed in the United States of America
02 01 00   5 4 3 2 1

Library of Congress Cataloging-in-Publication Data

Lancaster, Carol.
  Transforming foreign aid: United States assistance in the 21st century / Carol Lancaster.
    p. cm.
  Includes bibliographical references and index.
  1. Economic assistance, American.
  2. Economic assistance, American—Developing countries. I. Institute for International Economics (U.S.) II. Title.
  HC60.L298   2000
  338.91′73—dc21
                                00-039659
  ISBN 0-88132-291-1

Contents

Preface   vii

Acknowledgments   xiii

Introduction   1

1   The Phenomenon of Foreign Aid   9
    What is Foreign Aid?   9
    How Much US Aid   10
    Other US Foreign Aid Programs   12
    Trends in US Aid   14
    US Aid in a World of Foreign Assistance   15
    Foreign Aid in Total Financial Flows   16

2   The Purposes and Organization of US Foreign Aid Today   17
    Purposes   17
    The Management of US Foreign Aid   28
    The Organization of US Foreign Aid   31
    Purposes, Organizations, and Programs:
        First Cut at a Matrix   32

3   The Politics of Foreign Aid   35
    The Budgetary Process and Foreign Aid   35
    Actors and Interactions   39
    Conclusion   54

4   US Foreign Aid in the Probable World of the 21ˢᵗ Century   57
    The Probable World of the New Century   57

Three Major Trends   58
Summing Up   85

5 Organizing for a New Century   **89**
The Organization of US Aid in the New Century   89
Getting From Here to There   94

Appendix A A Brief Description of Organizations
                Funded by US Aid   97
Appendix B Assumptions and Estimates for Aid Matrix   102

Index   **105**

Tables
Table 1.1 US foreign aid, 2000   11
Table 2.1 Organizations funded with US foreign aid   32
Table 2.2 US foreign aid matrix: Purposes, programs,
           organizations, and budget (fiscal year 1998)   33
Table 3.1 The budgetary process for foreign aid: USAID   36
Table 3.2 Child survival and disease programs
           as part of total Development Assistance   48
Table 4.1 Refugees and relief, 1991-98   60
Table 4.2 Projected world population   62
Table 4.3 Foreign direct investment in the developing world   77
Table 4.4 Economic growth in the developing world   78

Figures
Figure 1.1 US foreign aid, 1986-2000   14
Figure 1.2 Net official Development Assistance, 1990-98   16

Preface

At regular four-year intervals, books and articles that recommend reforming foreign aid are published. Such studies rarely examine US foreign aid in its totality—bilateral, multilateral, and assistance to international organizations. They usually accept as valid the existing purposes of foreign aid and focus primarily on issues of organization and funding levels. Many ignore the political context in which foreign aid decisions are made.

This study is different. Its approach is much more fundamental and its policy recommendations are more radical. It looks at *all* US foreign aid. It does *not* assume that the past purposes of aid—rhetorical or real—are those of the present or the future. It puts its analysis and recommendations on future purposes of foreign aid in a political context that emphasizes US interests and values, the role of Executive Branch agencies, the Congress, private groups and public opinion. It links recommended changes in the organization of US foreign aid to the purposes of that aid.

This study does *not* discuss funding levels for US foreign aid. The main reason is that the level of aid funding should derive from the purposes of that aid, which are the focus of this analysis. Moreover, when a study includes recommendations on the level of foreign aid funding, discussions inevitably focus on that single issue. It is the intent of this volume to contribute to a long overdue discussion and debate on the *purposes* of foreign aid.

Carol Lancaster finds that the purposes of US foreign aid today are different from those of the past half century and are even different from the way foreign aid is described by public officials today. "Security" has become "peacekeeping," and not just in the Middle East. "Humanitarian relief" remains an important purpose of US aid but its scope of operation has expanded with its growing use to deal with man-made disasters in various parts of the world.

The purposes of "development" aid, besides economic growth and poverty reduction in poor countries, now include transnational problems like infectious diseases and environmental crises, and what Lancaster calls "humane concerns"—helping disadvantaged groups abroad such as street children and victims of war. These new purposes are distinct in motivation and method from traditional notions of development (although they may have an impact on development as well). US aid is also being used to promote democracy and support economic and social transitions in former communist countries.

The current landscape of US foreign aid is cluttered. We have four bilateral aid agencies. We contribute to seven multilateral development banks and numerous UN organizations. Nearly every cabinet agency of the US government now has its own "foreign aid" program. The degree of overlap and the opportunities for incoherence have grown with the expansion of the number of aid-funded activities abroad and the variety of public agencies engaged in their funding.

The politics of US foreign aid have also begun to change. While both Democrat and Republican Congresses have cut foreign aid substantially during the past decade, there are certain purposes for which there is a substantial degree of bipartisan support: aid for peacemaking, as in Colombia; and aid for humanitarian relief, as in Kosovo or Central America (during Hurricane Mitch). Indeed, it is not yet well recognized that US foreign aid rose significantly during the final years of the 1990s (and that nearly all of the increases were for these two purposes). Another area of bipartisan support is addressing transnational problems and promoting humane concerns; over the last few years, Congress has legislated increasing the funding level for both these purposes as well.

Lancaster looks into the probable world of the 21st century as a first step to identifying the major purposes of future US aid. She finds that peacemaking will likely continue to make an important, and possibly rising, claim on US aid. Addressing transnational problems and humane concerns will also become major purposes. Humanitarian relief will remain widely supported by the US public and Congress. Development, as traditionally defined, will decline in importance, as will supporting democracy and economic and political transitions in Eastern Europe and the former Soviet Union. This combination of four major purposes not only reflects US interests and values in the new century but can provide a new basis for bipartisan support for the overall foreign aid program.

If the United States is to pursue these purposes effectively, it needs to rethink the organization of its aid program and the modalities by which aid is delivered. Lancaster recommends a substantial reorganization of US bilateral aid, reducing the number of agencies from four to two and aligning purposes with organization for all US assistance. She also urges a significant revision in the way US bilateral aid is delivered, making it far more flexible and shifting the major responsibility for designing and implementing aid-funded activities to the recipients of that aid, whether they be governments or private organizations.

This study is the most fundamental rethinking of US foreign aid to appear in print for some years. It will be controversial, and should help clarify the issues and offer recommendations on how the United States can address them. It will, in short, ask and try to answer the key question: How should the United States use its concessional resources abroad to support its interests and values in the 21st century?

The Institute for International Economics is a private nonprofit institution for the study and discussion of international economic policy. Its purpose is to analyze important issues in that area and develop and communicate practical new approaches for dealing with them. The Institute is completely nonpartisan.

The Institute is funded largely by philanthropic foundations. Major institutional grants are now being received from the William M. Keck, Jr. Foundation and the Starr Foundation. A number of other foundations and private corporations contribute to the highly diversified financial resources of the Institute. About 26 percent of the Institute's resources in our latest fiscal year were provided by contributors outside the United States, including about 11 percent from Japan. The Rockefeller Foundation provided generous financial support for this project.

The Board of Directors bears overall responsibility for the Institute and gives general guidance and approval to its research program—including the identification of topics that are likely to become important over the medium run (one to three years), and which should be addressed by the Institute. The Director, working closely with the staff and outside Advisory Committee, is responsible for the development of particular projects and makes the final decision to publish an individual study.

The Institute hopes that its studies and other activities will contribute to building a stronger foundation for international economic policy around the world. We invite readers of these publications to let us know how they think we can best accomplish this objective.

C. Fred Bergsten
Director
August 2000

Acknowledgments

It takes a village to write a book—someone to give you shelter, someone to fund your research, elders and friends to give advice, and family to provide encouragement. I want to thank a number of the members of my village who made this book possible. I am grateful to the Rockefeller Foundation for funding the research. A special thanks to Foundation officers, Robert Herdt and Steve Sinding, for their support. Heartfelt thanks to Fred Bergsten and others at the Institute for International Economics for giving me a place to do the research and writing, advice in shaping it up, patience while it was being written and, most importantly, for publishing it. This is my fourth book written at the Institute. I am deeply appreciative of repeated opportunities to work at one of the best policy research institutes anywhere, anytime.

A number of people were kind enough to read this manuscript and make very helpful comments—Brian Atwood, Gordon Adams, Per Pinstrup-Anderson, Rodney Bent, Elliot Berg, Michael Feldstein, Tom Fox, David Gordon, Catherine Gwin, Bryan Hehir, George Ingram, Craig Johnstone, Brad Langmaid, Princeton Lyman, Walter North, Larry Nowels, Bill Reese, Vernon Ruttan, William Scheurch, John Sewell, Todd Stewart, Jennifer Whitaker, Casimir Yost, Isiah Frank, James Michel, Jennifer Ward, and several anonymous reviewers. Not everyone liked the form or content of this book but each, with his or her criticisms and suggestions, helped to make it better. None can be blamed for any shortcomings. Those belong to me.

I had research assistance from Jennifer Harhigh, Kim Cook, Gargee Ghosh, and Sarah Bannerjee—all from the Georgetown University MSFS Program—for which I am grateful.

Finally, I must thank my husband, Curt Farrar, for reading yet another manuscript and giving valuable suggestions and, together with my son, Doug, for putting up with the many evenings, weekends and holidays when I was occupied with researching and writing this book. I confess I am also grateful for their shared obsession with soccer.

Introduction

How should the US government spend its concessional resources abroad to support its interests and values in the new century? Are the purposes, programs, and organization of US aid in the 20th century relevant to the challenges and opportunities of the 21st? Is there a new policy paradigm that can serve as a basis for the political support required to sustain foreign assistance in future years? These questions have confronted the United States since the end of the Cold War and have yet to be satisfactorily answered. They are the focus of this book.

This book is not the first attempt to address the future of US foreign aid. The issue has regularly arisen every decade—often with each change of administration. But since the end of the Cold War, there has been a succession of studies recommending substantial changes in foreign aid. In December 1992, the Overseas Development Council (ODC) published its white paper, entitled *Reinventing Foreign Aid*, which focused entirely on reforming the US Agency for International Development (USAID), proposing that a new "Sustainable Development Cooperation Agency" be established to address issues of human development, environment, and democracy. In 1996, ODC and the Henry L. Stimson Center published a report by Catherine Gwin, David Gordon, and Steve Sinding, entitled *What Future for US Aid?*, which found that the development mission of USAID could be more effectively achieved if it were seen as more central to US foreign policy interests generally. It recommended that USAID be reorganized, with the policy function placed in the Department of State and the implementation of aid-funded projects and programs organized in a new public foundation. In that same year, Vernon Ruttan published a book, *United States Development Assistance Policy*, in which he recommended that USAID be abolished and replaced with several independent US government institutes to provide foreign assistance for scientific, technical, and economic cooperation; voluntary cooperation; and regional development activities in various parts of the world.

In 1996, Lawrence Eagleburger and Robert Barry published an article in *Foreign Affairs* urging that USAID be merged into the Department of State for better coordination of US foreign policy. Earlier that year, in the same journal, Paul Kennedy, Robert Chase, and Emily Hill argued in their article "Pivotal States" that US aid should be concentrated on a limited number of regionally influential states to address transnational and other issues. (This controversial article, later expanded into a book entitled *The Pivotal States*, was one of the few on foreign aid that focused on purpose rather than organizational changes.)

In the following year, Michael O'Hanlon and Carol Graham published a study, *A Half Penny on the Federal Dollar: The Future of Development Aid*, in which they urged that US development aid had been relatively ineffective, that it should be concentrated on promoting economic growth, that it should be provided selectively to governments with strong economic policies, and that it should be increased substantially. Also in 1997, the Center for Strategic and International Studies (CSIS) published a study entitled *The United States and the Multilateral Development Banks*, which found that those banks did indeed support US interests in promoting global stability and prosperity abroad. The study identified a proliferation of functions and weakness in setting priorities or discarding unsuitable roles. It concluded by recommending greater selectivity in the lending operations of these organizations and expanding of US aid to the multilateral development banks and that the "convening" capacity of the banks (i.e., their ability to mobilize multilateral action on particular problems) should be more utilized.

In March 2000, another study of the World Bank and International Monetary Fund was published. This study, commissioned by Congress, was undertaken by an 11-person panel of scholars and experts appointed by Republican and Democratic members of Congress, not all of whom supported the study's findings. (A number of the Democrats dissented.) The study found that the Bank, the Fund, and the regional development banks had failed to lift poor countries out of poverty after half a century of lending and that there was considerable wasteful duplication among them. It recommended that all of these institutions restrict their activities to a more limited set of objectives. The Fund would lend only for short-term liquidity crises, and the Bank would eliminate lending altogether and restrict its aid to grants to the poorest countries, primarily in Africa. The regional development banks would take on primary responsibility for aid in Asia and Latin America. (The African Development Bank was seen as not yet ready for that responsibility.) These institutions would write off all loans to low-income, heavily indebted countries.

Two other studies are worth mentioning because they signal a growing attention to international public goods issues as a focus of foreign assistance. *Global Public Goods: International Cooperation in the 21st Century*, edited by Inge Kaul, Isabelle Grunberg, and Marc Stern, identifies worldwide threats to human well-being as a high priority for foreign aid in the new century. Such threats include international disease transmission, environmental degradation, crime, drugs, and terrorism. Another book making much of the same argument is *The Future of Development Assistance: Common Pools and International Public Goods*, by Ravi Kanbur and Todd Sandler (also published in 1999).[1]

This book builds on many of these works and draws on other studies, documents, and interviews, as well as my direct experience with US foreign aid, inside and outside government, during the past three decades. But it goes well beyond these studies in its focus, comprehensiveness and recommendations. It offers a fundamentally new vision of the role of US aid in the new century and recommends how to transform aid to fit that new vision.

A Vision of US Foreign Aid in the New Century

The world of the 21st century is one of great promise. The threats to global security and even to the survival of the human race abated with the end of the Cold War. The prospect of increasing prosperity resulting from technological advances and global economic integration are greater than any other time in history. Democratization in many countries, combined with the spread of information technology, has given a political voice to many who, deprived of freedom and information, have long been silent.

The 21st century has also brought many challenges—the challenge of making peace in the numerous civil conflicts that have erupted in

---

1. Overseas Development Council, *Reinventing Foreign Aid*, Washington: Overseas Development Council, 1992; Catherine Gwin, David Gordon, and Steve Sinding, *What Future for US Aid?* Washington: Overseas Development Council and Henry L. Stimson Center, 1996; Vernon Ruttan, *United States Development Assistance Policy*, Baltimore: Johns Hopkins University Press, 1996; Lawrence Eagleburger and Robert Barry, Dollars and Sense Diplomacy, *Foreign Affairs* 75, no. 3, 1996; Paul Kennedy, Robert Chase, and Emily Hill, The Pivotal States, *Foreign Affairs* 75, no. 1; Paul Kennedy, Robert Chase, and Emily Hill, *The Pivotal States: A New Framework for US Policy in the Developing World*, New York: Norton, 1998; Michael O'Hanlon and Carol Graham, *A Half Penny on the Federal Dollar*, Washington: Brookings Institution, 1997; CSIS, *The United States and the Multilateral Development Banks*, Washington, June 1998; Inge Kaul, Isabelle Grunberg, Marc A. Stern, eds., *Global Public Goods: International Cooperation in the 21st Century*, New York: Oxford University Press (for United Nations Development Program), 1999; Ravi Kanbur with Kevin M. Morrison, *The Future of Development Assistance: Common Pools and International Public Goods*, Washington: Overseas Development Council, Policy Essay no. 25, 1995.

Africa, Europe, and the newly independent states of the former Soviet Union; the challenge of dealing with transnational issues, which have gained urgency with increasing world population, prosperity, and integration; and the challenge of ensuring that the negative consequences of globalization are managed and mitigated. Further, the 21st century promises to be a period of rapid change and, at times, unanticipated emergencies—such as the Asian financial crisis or the violence in Kosovo—that require a quick and effective international response to contain and resolve.

The United States remains the sole global superpower of the 21st century. Its leadership will be essential to address many of the challenges and crises of that world, especially those that threaten important US interests. Among those challenges will be peacemaking in regions of particular interest to the United States—Europe, the Middle East, the Pacific Rim, and near its own borders—especially where effective arrangements do not exist to help resolve conflict. Addressing the transnational problems that arise from a prosperous, populous, integrating world will be another set of challenges requiring US leadership.

Infectious diseases break out on one country and now quickly spread across borders to affect Americans at home. The loss of biodiversity in Africa or Latin America affects the future availability of food and medicine in the United States. A shortage of water in the Middle East fuels tensions there and lead to wars that touch Americans, both through their ties of affinity and with the impact on oil prices, through their pocketbooks. Some of these transnational problems can be anticipated; others cannot. But it seems likely that they will bulk large in the world of the new century and in the demands on US leadership.

Foreign aid will continue to be an important tool of US foreign policy in the new century. But its major purposes will be different from those of the past half-century. They will follow the issues described above—aid for peacemaking; aid to address transnational problems; aid for humanitarian relief; and aid to address humane concerns, such as bringing direct help to children, poor women, and other deprived and vulnerable groups abroad. (Foreign assistance will continue to be allocated to promoting economic and social development, and democracy. But these will have less priority now than in previous decades because of the economic progress in much of the world, and the transition to democracy and free markets in most former socialist countries and elsewhere.)

These four major purposes of US aid in the new century provide the basis for a new policy paradigm for US assistance. Like the old paradigm, which combined security (containing communism) and development, this paradigm is a mix of both US interests and values. Properly presented and explained by the president, it can provide the foundation for a new constituency for foreign aid. Indeed, that constituency is already beginning to take shape, for Congress has increasingly directed the administration to allocate an increasing portion of US bilateral aid to transnational problems and child survival.

The purposes of US aid in the new century argue for a reshaping of the organization and management of that aid. US bilateral aid should be reconfigured with assistance for purposes central to US diplomacy—peace-making, addressing transnational issues, and promoting democracy—located in the Department of State with the capacity to manage the implementation as well as the policies governing those activities. Bilateral aid for humanitarian relief (now located in USAID and the Department of State) and for humane concerns would be housed in a new aid agency, which would absorb the two small government foundations (InterAmerican Foundation and African Development Foundation) doing community development work, together with the elements of USAID that provide aid for these purposes. US aid for economic and social development—the main focus of which would be in Africa and a handful of other very poor countries—would be channeled primarily through the multilateral development banks, and a portion of US aid to address transnational issues (i.e., technical assistance) would be allocated to those international organizations with the capacity to address those issues effectively. This division among bilateral aid, aid for multilateral development banks, and aid for international organizations is based on a logical division of labor among these various types of institutions. Mission creep on the part of many of them has blurred their current focus.

Finally, a word needs to be said about the management of US bilateral aid. Aid for transnational issues will present a new management challenge to future administrations, because most US government agencies have established their own aid programs abroad. The increasing engagement of all parts of the US government—in effect its "globalization"—in providing technical assistance and training to its counterparts in foreign governments is a striking phenomenon of the last decade of the 20th century, and one likely to become more pronounced in the 21st. Future administrations will want to find ways to exploit as well as coordinate this change.

A second management challenge for US bilateral aid is for the US government to expand the growing opportunities to collaborate with private enterprises, foundations, and nongovernmental organizations (NGOs) in the funding of aid-supported activities abroad. This collaboration requires that all parties bring resources to the table and work together to fund agreed-upon activities. The recent commitment by a number of pharmaceutical companies, US government agencies, and the World Bank, to develop vaccines for use in poor countries is one example of this type of collaboration. There are likely to be many more such opportunities in the future for aid agencies flexible and innovative enough to identify and exploit them.

Similarly, more collaborative relationships with those organizations—

governments and NGOs—receiving US aid also make sense. The elaborate strategic programming processes and large field missions associated with US bilateral aid in the past no longer make sense in a world where the amount of bilateral aid is relatively small and where recipients of that aid can and should take far more responsibility for designing and implementing aid-funded activities than in the past. In short, flexibility and creativity will be among the key qualities of US aid, especially for humane concerns, in the future.

Some of the changes proposed here are already visible in US aid programs, which are beginning in an ad hoc fashion to adapt to the world of the new century. But what is required is not an ad hoc adjustment to a greatly altered international environment but a set of coherent purposes, programs, and organizational and management changes that would transform US foreign aid to bring it into line with US interests and values in the probable world of the 21st century.

The Plan of This Book

In addition to offering a new vision for US foreign aid, this book also offers an analysis of US aid as it is today—its definition, purposes, organization, management, and politics. Chapters 1, 2, and 3 cover these topics. Chapters 4 and 5 outline in detail the purposes, organization, and management of US aid in the probable world of the new century. What this book does *not* do is recommend particular budgetary levels for future foreign assistance programs. Such levels are set not only on the basis of the purposes of aid, and the challenges and opportunities it is intended to address but also with regard to broader considerations, including fiscal policy and other demands on discretionary budgetary resources, topics beyond the scope of this study. Further, including recommendations on foreign aid levels would almost surely focus the attention of readers on that topic (as it usually does) and the far more important questions of purpose would be neglected.

In writing this book, I have assumed (on the basis of past research and experience) that foreign aid can be effective in realizing both US interests and values abroad and should continue to be an essential tool in US foreign policy.[2] However, I have also tried to analyze foreign aid

---

2. There is a lively debate on the effectiveness of aid in promoting development abroad. See, e.g., World Bank, *Assessing Aid* (Washington: World Bank, 1998) or my book, *Aid in Africa*, Chicago: University of Chicago Press, 1999. Among the important findings of these and numerous other examinations of aid effectiveness is that aid can be effective where the policy and institutional environment in recipient countries is supportive of development and where aid projects and programs are managed properly, but that has not always been the case. The debate on where and how aid is effective is an important one, but it takes us well beyond the scope of this study.

in as dispassionate a manner as possible, not assuming that the tasks and organizations of the past five decades are necessarily appropriate to the world of the new century. I realize that many will disagree with the analysis and findings in this book. (Indeed, many already have from reading it in its various drafts.) Some will find it wrongheaded; others, too radical; and still others, not radical enough. Whatever its limitations, it will have accomplished its main purpose if it leads to a better informed debate on US foreign aid.

1

The Phenomenon of Foreign Aid

What Is Foreign Aid?

Foreign aid is often used to refer to a wide variety of resource transfers. Some think of any transfer of public funds abroad—including military expenditures or trade financing—as foreign aid. Others think of it only as humanitarian relief for victims of disasters. In fact, foreign aid has an official meaning. According to the Development Assistance Committee (DAC) of the Organization for Economic Cooperation and Development (OECD), foreign aid (or Official Development Assistance) is the transfer abroad of public resources on concessional terms (with at least a 25 percent grant element), a significant objective of which is to bring about an improvement in economic, political, or social conditions in developing countries. This definition—expanded to apply to concessional resource transfers, one objective of which is to improve economic, social, and political conditions in any foreign country—is the one we shall use for the purposes of this study.[1] It does not include military expenditures or mili-tary aid, trade or investment financing, public funding for cultural exchanges, expenditures on foreign intelligence gathering or covert action, or government-to-government loans at market rates of interest. Funding for anti-drug or anti-terrorism activities abroad, international peacekeeping operations, or efforts to stop the spread of weapons of mass

---

1. The practical difference in these definitions is that the DAC excludes concessional resource transfers to the better-off countries of Eastern Europe, the former Soviet Union, and Israel. We shall include these transfers, which are significant in size, in our calculations of US aid.

destruction are not included in the DAC definition of foreign aid, although they are often lumped together with that aid in the public mind and, at times, in the statements of government officials. We shall note the size and importance of such flows here but not include them in our overall definition and data on foreign aid.

US foreign aid is provided largely as grants to international organizations, foreign governments, or NGOs. In 2000, of an overall aid level of $9.4 billion, just over $1.4 billion, or 14 percent, was planned as contributions to multilateral development banks and international organizations. Detailed data are not available on the proportion of US bilateral aid channeled through NGOs, but USAID officials have estimated that about a third of the nearly $2 billion Development Assistance funds are implemented by NGOs. US aid is used to fund relief activities, investment projects, technical advice and training, and balance of payments and budgetary support—the latter two are usually termed "program" aid. Aid can also be provided in kind rather than in cash or credits, in the form of food, medicine, or other commodities.

How Much US Aid?

The $9.4 billion in US foreign aid in 2000 was appropriated to the agencies and programs listed in table 1.1.[2]

US bilateral economic assistance programs include Development Assistance, intended primarily to promote economic and social progress in recipient countries; Economic Support Fund (ESF) monies, used mainly in support of diplomatic purposes (e.g., peacemaking in the Middle East); food aid (called Public Law 480 (PL 480)) primarily for disaster relief and nutrition intervention in poor countries; programs in Eastern Europe and the former Soviet Union to support economic and political transitions in those countries; funding for the Peace Corps, which sends US volunteers who usually work in communities in poor countries or countries in transition to help improve social and economic conditions there, and for the African Development Foundation and the InterAmerican Foundation, which work on community improvement and empowerment in their respective regions. USAID has policy leadership in Development Assistance and food aid and manages the implementation of those programs as well as the ESF and aid in Eastern Europe and the former Soviet Union. US contributions to and participation in multilateral development banks are managed by the Department of Treasury. The Department of State manages funding for international organizations and programs for refugees.

---

2. The data included in table 1.1 cover voluntary contributions made by the United States to international organizations and programs. The United States also makes assessed contributions to such programs, amounting to $880 million in 2000. Only a proportion of

Table 1.1   US foreign aid, 2000 (millions of US dollars)

Type of aid	
Bilateral	
Development Assistance	2,008
Economic Support Fund	2,792
Food aid	800
Eastern Europe and former Soviet Union	1,369
Debt relief	123
InterAmerican Foundation and African Development Foundation	19
Peace Corps	245
State Department Refugee Program	623
Multilateral	
World Bank	811
Inter-American Development Bank and Investment Corporation	43
Asian Development Bank and Fund	91
African Development Bank and Fund	131
European Bank for Reconstruction and Development	36
International organizations and programs	283
Total	**9,374**

Note: The data in this chart do not include USAID's operating expenses ($520 million) and other overhead costs. The funds included in "International organizations and programs" are voluntary contributions only and mainly go to the United Nations Development Program, UNICEF, and other agencies.

Source: The numbers used here are drawn from USAID's "Congressional Presentation 2001," http://www.info.usaid.gov/press/releases/2000/budget2001.html, supplemented with details from the US Department of State's "Summary and Highlights FY2001 International Affairs (Function 150) Budget Request," http://www.state.gov/www/budget/numbers_full.html#2001. These documents include actual appropriations for FY 2000. Obligations and disbursements of aid may vary somewhat from appropriated levels.

Not included in these numbers are funds spent abroad to fight drugs, crime, and prevent the spread of nuclear weapons. US government expenditures (managed by the Department of State) for these purposes were set at $520 million in 2000, and the Clinton administration planned to request a further supplemental from Congress for Plan Colombia (to fight drugs and violence there) of $818 million. One could also include the funds spent on several private institutes and foundations, including the Asia Foundation, the North South Institute, the East West Institute, and the National Endowment for Democracy, which would add just over $50 million to this total. They are not normally included in foreign aid data, and so they were not included here.[3]

---

these agencies provides what could be considered as foreign aid under the definition used here, and much of the US contribution is used for overhead. See http://www.state.gov.

3. Ibid.

Other US Foreign Aid Programs

There is reason to believe that table 1.1 underestimates US government expenditures on foreign aid as defined here—perhaps by a considerable amount. A 1994 study by the Office of Management and Budget (OMB) found that domestic US government agencies requested $1 billion in appropriations (slightly up from the level in 1993), to fund technical assistance and training for foreign nationals.[4] There have been no studies updating these numbers, and US domestic government agencies do not usually classify their expenditures according to foreign versus domestic activities. But anecdotal evidence and an examination of the Web sites of most US domestic agencies suggest that these foreign aid programs (though they are never termed such by the agencies) have continued, almost certainly expanded, and increasingly become institutionalized with the establishment of international divisions or bureaus. For example, the Department of the Treasury provides advice to foreign governments on taxes and customs laws and administration (and has a line item in its fiscal 2000 budget for $1.5 million to fund those services). The Department of Justice provides help on strengthening the judiciaries of foreign countries. The Departments of Transportation, Agriculture, Commerce, Labor, Interior, Energy, and Health and Human Services (HHS) and the Environmental Protection Agency (EPA) also have their own programs of foreign assistance relating to their particular portfolios, involving mainly the provision of technical assistance and training to foreign nationals. Finally, the Departments of State and Defense fund concessional expenditures abroad in the areas of humanitarian relief.

It is worth spending a moment examining what has given rise to the establishment of foreign aid programs by federal government agencies whose focus has traditionally been primarily domestic. Many of these agencies have long had international responsibilities. The Labor Department, for instance, has had the lead in representing the United States at the International Labor Organization. The HHS Department has had a major role in US participation in the World Health Organization (WHO). What appears to be new is the technical assistance and training offered by these agencies to foreign governments. The programs are in part a response to the "globalization" of US domestic policies: Acting globally is increasingly becoming essential for dealing with local problems. One

---

4. Office of Management and Budget, "International Activities of US Government Agencies," draft, 1994 (part of NSC/PRD-20). This report was never published. Domestic US government agencies actually implement larger "aid" programs abroad than these figures would suggest, because USAID transfers some of its funds to them to finance technical assistance and other development-related activities in foreign countries. Several foreign governments—e.g., the government of Saudi Arabia—have also "bought" technical assistance from various US government agencies, which further increases the overall size of these agencies' expenditures abroad.

recognition of the globalization of US domestic policies is reflected in a recent statement by the EPA that "international cooperation is critical to achieving EPA's mission," including ". . . reducing global, regional and transboundary risks that directly affect health and environment in the United States."[5] Other US government agencies have clearly come to similar conclusions. Another sign of the impact of globalization on the US government is the appointment of the HHS secretary to a seat on the National Security Council (NSC) in her agency's role as a lead on issues of bio-terrorism.

Another spur to the establishment of foreign aid programs in most US government agencies has been the end of the Cold War. With the collapse of communist regimes in Eastern Europe and the former Soviet Union in 1991, the United States initiated aid programs in most of these countries, with funding managed mainly by USAID. But because USAID had no presence in these countries and there were few private organizations experienced in working there, much of the aid from USAID was channeled through other US government agencies to give new governments advice on tax regimes; judicial reform; commercial, civil, and criminal law; and environmental regulations. These activities in former socialist bloc countries moved domestic US government agencies directly into international aid activities. Not surprisingly, once they had established programs abroad and allocated staff to manage them, the agencies made an effort to continue these programs even after USAID funding channeled through them decreased, by allocating their own funds for such activities.

Another important factor stimulating domestic agencies to create aid programs abroad appears to have been the binational commissions set up under the Clinton administration and headed by Vice President Al Gore. Five such commissions have been created—one each with the governments of Egypt, Kazakhstan, Russia, South Africa, and the Ukraine. These commissions, which meet twice yearly, are made up of cabinet secretaries who cochair committees with their counterparts in the partner governments to examine problems in their particular areas of responsibility and come up with programs to address them. These programs, or deliverables, usually require funding, some of which typically comes from the budgets of the agencies themselves and some from USAID or the Department of State.

The dozens of US government agencies active in Egypt, Russia, and South Africa reflect the pressures generated by these commissions. A similar dynamic is at work whenever the president travels abroad with cabinet officers. (Including cabinet officers in these trips now appears to be a common practice, judging from the official delegations traveling with President Clinton to Africa, China, and other countries.) They typically meet with their counterparts in the countries being visited to

---

5. See http://www.epa.gov. Environmental Protection Agency, April 1998.

Figure 1.1 US foreign aid, 1986-2000

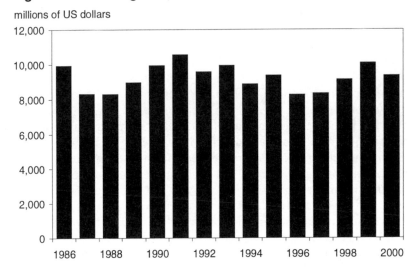

millions of US dollars

discuss issues of common interest and frequently to announce new programs.

A final reason—often cited by government officials themselves—for the proliferation of foreign aid programs in domestic US government agencies is that cabinet officers find international travel and work attractive because it is often less stressful or politically contentious than the domestic issues they must spend most of their time addressing, and they like to back up their increasing penchant for travel and work abroad with resources.

The globalization of domestic policies and politics suggests that these programs are likely to continue and grow in the future.

Trends in US Aid

Figure 1.1 shows the trends in US aid (excluding aid from domestic agencies) from 1986 to 2000. From nearly $10 billion in 1986 (which included a special supplement of ESF for Israel and emergency food aid in the wake of the Ethiopian famine), aid levels dropped until 1989, when they began to rise again, with new aid programs in Nicaragua and Panama in the aftermath of political changes in those countries. Aid reached a peak in 1991, with increases for drought-stricken countries of Africa and former socialist countries in Eastern Europe, and a rise in US contributions to several multilateral development banks. Aid levels dropped in 1994, as a Democratic Congress cut government expenditures in an effort to balance the budget, and dropped again sharply in 1996 and 1997 with the new, Republican-controlled Congress. In 1998, US aid levels rose after Congress agreed to appropriate funds to clear nearly $400 million US arrears to the World Bank. In 1999, there was a $2 billion spike in US foreign aid, raising it to $11.1 billion. This increase was almost entirely for disaster assistance to Central America and for Kosovo refugees. The total aid for fiscal 2000 (as of May 2000) fell back to just under $9.4 billion. This amount included $450 million to fulfill US commitments under the Wye River Agreement between Israel and the Palestinians. (Along with the foreign aid budget request to Congress for 2001 was a supplemental request for 2000 of $1.2 billion for Plan Colombia, further expenditures in Kosovo, and additional funding for debt restructuring.) Clearly, the elimination of the budget deficit has eased pressures to cut foreign aid generally. It is important to note, however, that most of the increases since 1998 have been for humanitarian relief and peacemaking. Apart from funding to clear past arrears in US commitments to the World Bank, aid for long-term development programs has increased by a relatively small amount. And Development Assistance funding remained lower in 2000 than in 1988.

US Aid in a World of Foreign Assistance

The DAC compiles annual data on foreign aid from its member states.[6] Japan is the largest aid donor, at $10.6 billion, with the United States in second place, at $8.8 billion. As a percentage of gross national product, aid from Norway is the largest, amounting to nearly one percent in 1998. Aid from the United States is the smallest, amounting to 0.1 percent in the same year. Trends in aid-giving show that total aid worldwide declined from a peak of $61 billion in 1992 to $52 billion in 1998. The largest decrease was a nearly $4 billion drop in Japanese aid between 1995 and 1998. (Japanese aid had risen sharply before then.) The second largest drop was a $3 billion real fall in US aid between 1992 and 1998. Canadian, German, French, and Italian aid levels have all declined since 1992. Only the United Kingdom and a number of smaller European countries have increased their aid since that year. It is worth noting that after 5 years of decline, foreign aid worldwide increased slightly in 1998. It is not yet clear whether this was a trend or a hiccup. (See figure 1.2).

---

6. DAC members include Australia, Austria, Belgium, Canada, Denmark, Finland, France, Germany, Greece, Ireland, Italy, Japan, Luxembourg, The Netherlands, New Zealand, Norway, Portugal, Spain, Switzerland, the United Kingdom, and the United States. The data in this section are drawn from the DAC, Development Cooperation 1999 Report, OECD, Paris 2000.

Figure 1.2 Net official development assistance, 1990-98

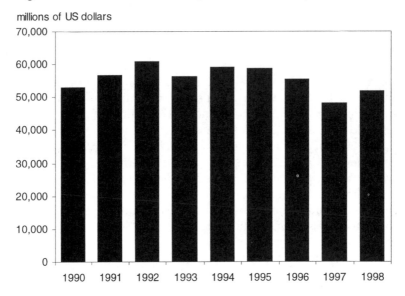

millions of US dollars

Foreign Aid in Total Financial Flows

One final point needs to be made to set the stage for the analysis in the following chapters. The decline in foreign aid during the past decade has occurred in conjunction with a dramatic increase in private financial flows. From $53 billion in 1993, private flows to developing countries increased to $147 billion in 1998. They had risen to $292 billion in 1996 before the Asian financial crisis and have since fallen. What has not decreased, however, has been the level of foreign direct investment (FDI), which reached $118 billion in 1998, up from $70 billion in 1996. Much of this investment has been concentrated in a dozen or so countries, including Brazil and China. (For further details, see chapter 5.) But many other developing countries have benefited from a substantial increase in FDI as well.

FDI is not a substitute for foreign aid. Foreign investors are usually reluctant to invest in basic infrastructure (e.g., rural roads), primary education, basic research on problems related to poor countries (e.g., malaria cures), providing for international public goods, offsetting market failures, providing relief, or helping the needy. But foreign aid can help create the preconditions that encourage foreign investment and enable governments both to finance and manage their own investment without resorting to aid. Thus, for the many developing countries that have made good progress in creating the basic infrastructure and social services necessary to underpin their economic and social progress, and have the policy and institutional environment that private investors demand, the rise in FDI is good news indeed.

2

The Purposes, Management, and Organization of US Foreign Aid Today

An old Swahili proverb says that to arrive at your destination, you must know from whence you start. This chapter will examine from whence we start—that is, the purposes, management, and organization of US foreign aid as they are at the beginning of the new century. Purposes are defined here as the broad objectives of US bilateral and multilateral aid, which are used both to justify the aid to Congress and the public and to determine where the aid is spent and what sorts of activities it funds. (Justifications for aid that do not also influence the allocation and use of that aid are not included as purposes here, though several will be mentioned at the end of this section.)

Purposes

US foreign aid in 2000 is different from what it was just 10 years ago. There are six identifiable purposes of US aid. Three of them—promoting security, supporting development, and providing humanitarian relief—have existed for the past 5 decades. Whereas the words used by policymakers to describe these three purposes have remained the same, the substance of each has changed significantly in the past 10 years. In addition, three other purposes have gained in prominence in the past decade—supporting economic and political transitions in former socialist countries,

addressing transnational problems, and promoting democracy abroad.[1]
Let us examine these six purposes in detail.

Promoting Security

US aid was long justified by government officials and foreign policy elite
as an important instrument for protecting US security by helping contain
the expansion of communist influence. This motivation was most evident
in aid to Greece and Turkey, and the Marshall Plan in the late 1940s and
early 1950s; South Korea and other countries on the periphery of China,
and the Soviet Union in the 1950s; the Alliance for Progress in Latin
America in the 1960s; Indochina in the 1960s and early 1970s; the Horn of
Africa and Southern Africa in the 1970s and early 1980s; and Central
American countries in the mid-to-late 1980s. The bilateral aid program
intended primarily to support US security interests abroad was the ESF,
known earlier as Security Supporting Assistance. The security rationale
provided a general and often compelling justification for US foreign aid as
a whole because aid for development and other purposes, it was argued,
also promoted US security.

In reality, beginning in the mid-1970s and especially after the Camp
David Accords between Israel and Egypt in 1979, peacemaking began to
compete with the Cold War competition as the core focus of US bilateral
economic assistance for security purposes. Since 1979, nearly four-fifths
of ESF monies—typically $2 billion out of a total of around $2.5 billion
annually—have in fact been allocated to Israel and Egypt as an incentive
for them to maintain peace in the region. (In 1998, Congress and the
administration agreed to begin reducing the annual level of aid transfers
to these two countries with the aim of eliminating economic assistance
to Israel and reducing by half aid to Egypt over a 10-year period.) Other
funding for peacemaking has included aid to Cyprus, Jordan, Northern
Ireland, and more recently, Bosnia and other Balkan countries and the
West Bank/Gaza. (Aid for West Bank/Gaza and Jordan increased in 1999
and 2000 as a result of the Wye River Agreement between Israel and the
Palestinians.) Programs for Cambodia and Haiti can also be classified as
peacemaking—aimed at creating the conditions for internal peace and
stability in the wake of conflict or severe political disruption. In both
these countries, the United States took an active role in bringing about

---

1. None of these three purposes is entirely new to foreign aid. The United States provided aid in support of the political transition in Portugal in the 1970s. (I thank Brad
Langmaid for pointing this out.) It has for several decades put aid funds into population
and family planning programs—a transnational issue and usually viewed as such by
USAID's program managers—and democracy promotion was part of the aims of the
Alliance for Progress in the 1960s. But, with the exception of family planning, these
programs remained relatively small and limited in duration. That is no longer the case
today.

political change or a resolution of existing conflict. Foreign aid has become an important tool for consolidating those achievements.

Promoting Development

If the meaning of security as a purpose of foreign aid has shifted during the past several decades, the meaning of development and ideas about how to achieve it have changed even more, particularly in the past 10 years.

From the very beginning of the postwar period, the core objective of economic development was to help poor countries regarded as too impoverished to support their own rapid economic progress, grow, and thus reduce their poverty. Growth, in turn, required investment. With savings very low and international capital limited and wary of poor countries during the early decades after World War II, foreign aid was seen as a tool for raising investment levels. Further, such aid was regarded as especially appropriate for expanding infrastructure and promoting social development—that is, education, health, and other services that benefited all members of society—which were likely to be unattractive to private investors. In addition to helping fill investment gaps (and foreign exchange gaps), aid could provide the technical assistance and training that would expand the capacity of developing countries to manage their own economies. Finally, aid could also fund the research—especially in agriculture and health—that would address the particular needs of poor countries (again, with their limited markets, such research was unlikely to be of interest to major private investors) and thereby help them expand their productivity and prosperity.

This basic approach to using aid to promote development has continued until the present, with some important amendments. Aid was used in the 1970s for basic human needs—to fund investments by governments directly benefiting their poor when it was thought that economic growth was failing to reach the poor or making their lives more difficult. Aid shifted in the 1980s back to supporting growth (which, research has now shown, does, in fact, benefit the poor[2]), but in this case, it emphasized funding of essential economic reforms if private investment was to rise and lead to faster growth. Throughout all these changes and amendments in development thinking, the focus of aid and development was on bringing about beneficial economic and social change in particular countries, providing the capital that would not otherwise be available and the technical assistance essential for effective economic management in those countries.

---

2. Catherine Gwin and Ivan Nelson, *Perspectives on Aid and Development*, Overseas Development Council Policy Essay 22, Washington, 1997.

The 1990s brought a fundamental but little recognized change in the development community of what development was and the role of aid in it. The notion of development fragmented into three different concepts: One is the traditional, country-focused approach described above; one now refers to addressing transnational issues and problems; and one involves what we shall term "humane concerns."[3]

Humane concerns is used here to refer to aid provided (usually through NGOs) directly to disadvantaged communities or vulnerable groups to help improve the quality of their lives. Examples of this type of aid include assistance for poor children (e.g., inoculations or oral rehydration therapy), poor women (e.g., through micro-enterprise lending), AIDS orphans and street children, counseling victims of torture, prosthetics for those maimed by mines, and a variety of other community improvements. Much of this type of aid—if it is large enough and effective—can support development as traditionally conceived. But its motivation and management typically involve less a strategic intervention in another society aimed at bringing about broadly based economic and social change than simple altruism—a desire to help directly those in need who cannot help themselves.

We do not know how much US aid falls into this category at present. But one indication of its importance is the percentage of US Development Assistance channeled through NGOs, roughly 30 percent, as mentioned above. Another indication is the amount of aid earmarked by Congress for child survival—over $600 million in 2000 for a variety of activities intended to benefit children. These indicators suggest that aid for humane concerns is already sizable and is on the increase.

Transnational problems—arising from events or conditions in one country or region that adversely affect people in other countries—are not new. They have been present since national borders were created and people began crossing them. However, they have expanded in scope and accelerated in intensity with increasing world population and prosperity, and especially with the integrative process called globalization.

Many of these transnational problems are familiar ones. Like rapid population growth or international food insecurity, they have long been part of the discourse on development and the focus of aid interventions. But the way they are increasingly being viewed—as issues involving international public goods potentially affecting Americans rather than obstacles to economic progress in poor countries—is quite new.[4]

---

3. Others have defined development in still different terms, See, for example, Amartya Sen, *Development at Freedom*, New York: Knopf, 1999.

4. See, e.g., Inge Kaul, Isabelle Grunberg, and Marc A. Stern, eds., *Global Public Goods: International Cooperation in the 21st Century*, New York: Oxford University Press (for UNDP, 1999), and Ravi Kanbur with Kevin M. Morrison, *The Future of Development Assistance: Common Pools and International Public Goods*, Overseas Development Council Policy Essay no. 25, Washington, 1999.

Addressing transnational issues requires a different approach from that associated with aid to promote development. First of all, aid allocated to address a global problem should be provided to countries contributing the most to the problem and unable (or unwilling) to deal with it. Economic need and performance—key criteria for allocating traditional Development Assistance—are much less important. Second, aid will be allocated to address a particular problem in a country or group of countries rather than to bring about broad economic, social, and political change in countries receiving the aid. Thus the strategic orientation of this approach is global rather than country-focused, although working on transnational issues involves addressing the conditions or policies in particular localities that contribute to transnational problems.

The rising importance of transnational issues as a focus of US foreign aid is already evident in congressional action, in the statements of administration officials, and in the aid programs themselves. For fiscal 2000, for example, Congress passed legislation requiring the administration to spend $75 million on an Infectious Diseases Initiative to address the problems of tuberculosis, malaria, and yellow fever. The administration proposed a major boost in aid in 2000 to address the problems of HIV/AIDS, another major transnational issue. (HIV/AIDS has become so serious a problem—especially in Africa—that it is a development and humanitarian issue, producing 11 million orphans. It has even been described by the president as a US security issue.)

The rise of transnational problems as a focus of US diplomacy is evident in the creation in 1993 within the Department of State of a new post of undersecretary for global issues. USAID also has a Bureau of Global Issues. And, as noted above, a number of US government agencies (e.g., Department of HHS, EPA, and Department of Energy) now fund their own activities abroad, most of which address transnational problems.

Humanitarian Relief

The United States has long provided relief in cases of disasters abroad. In recent years, the United States has provided funding for relief from droughts, floods, epidemics, cyclones, hurricanes and typhoons, earthquakes, fires, mudslides, volcanic eruptions, terrorist attacks, and civil conflicts. This purpose of US foreign aid has long been the least controversial and the most supported by the American public, especially when human suffering resulting from such disasters has been viewed nationally on television.

During the past half a century, most of the humanitarian interventions undertaken by the US government have been primarily in poor countries unable to adequately finance their own relief efforts, although such interventions have also been undertaken in well-off countries when the disaster is a major one and when US expertise in various aspects of disaster relief is needed.

As with the other traditional purposes of US aid, the nature of US assistance in humanitarian crises has changed significantly during the past 10 years. Until the mid-1980s, disasters requiring aid from the United States and other governments were primarily natural disasters, as with the drought and famine in Ethiopia. Since the late 1980s, there has been a dramatic rise in man-made or complex disasters—mainly deriving from conflicts within countries—including those in Angola, Bosnia, Burundi, Liberia, and others, particularly in Africa. From a low of two or three complex disasters per year in 1985 and 1986, the number rose to 10 in 1989, and to 20 or more every year since then, save two years. In 1998, the natural and man-made disasters to which the United States responded with relief assistance reached 87.[5]

Complex crises typically present much greater challenges for humanitarian response than do natural disasters. They tend to be prolonged, continuing at times for decades. They create large numbers of refugees and displaced people and require humanitarian intervention while the conflict is ongoing as well as after it ceases. They are highly destructive of life and property, often over a wide area. And with the now common practice on the part of combatants of planting millions of mines, the threat to human life and economic recovery continues for many decades after the war, as in the cases of Cambodia and Mozambique.

Civil conflicts also frequently destroy political institutions and social comity, removing the local governmental partners necessary for rapid and effective humanitarian intervention, as in the case of southern Somalia or southern Sudan. Finally, to help war-torn societies recover from complex crises, humanitarian organizations are now challenged to help recreate the political institutions necessary to govern those societies. The rise in the number of complex crises thus has both increased the difficulties of humanitarian intervention by placing it at times in a physically dangerous and highly political environment and also extended the scope of that intervention to a whole new area of political and social reconstruction.

One of the results of the change in the nature of conflict over the past decade or so has been the creation by a number of US-supported aid agencies—USAID, the World Bank, and the United Nations Development Program (UNDP)—of new programs and bureaus to manage the complicated and still little understood tasks of helping countries emerging from crisis and conflict with reconstructing political institutions and

---

5. Of this total, 65 were natural disasters (up from 27 in 1997). See J. Brady Anderson [USAID administrator], Testimony before the House International Relations Committee, 15 March 2000. http://www.info.usaid.gov.

social reconciliation. USAID, in its major innovation of recent years, was the first to create such a program, housed in the new Office of Transition Initiatives. The World Bank subsequently established its Post-Conflict Unit. These programs include demining, demobilization and reintegration of combatants, support for political organization and elections, establishment of effective judicial systems (often including processes for prosecuting war crimes), and—in the words of the World Bank—aid for jump-starting the economy.[6]

With the rising importance of relief work and the expansion of relief efforts into the area of political and social reconstruction, both relief and development specialists have begun to emphasize the importance of linking relief to long-term development activities. There has been considerable discussion during the past several years on what the exact nature and extent of these linkages should be. An examination of this literature[7] points to a number of ways relief work can be made more consistent with development—for example, relief planners should try to ensure that victims of disaster remain at home if at all possible so they can begin economic activities as soon as the disaster is over; relief planners should undertake their activities with an understanding of the potential impact of their assistance on political and social conditions, especially in societies in conflict or emerging from conflict; and they should provide relief assistance while avoiding creating long-term dependence on that assistance. But what really comes out of the discussions of the links between relief and development, reflected in the initiatives of USAID, the World Bank, and others, is not so much the extent of those ties (which in fact appear limited) but the evolution of a new type of aid intervention—aid for political and social reconstruction. These interventions are not the short-term ones associated with traditional relief work, because they tend to continue over a longer period than interventions focused primarily on relieving human suffering. Further, they require a high degree of political and social knowledge and local experience on the part of external

---

6. See World Bank, *Supporting Peace: The World Bank's Role in Post-Conflict Reconstruction*, http://www.worldbank.org/html/extdr/backgrd/ibrd/peace.htm.

7. See, e.g., Simon Maxwell and Margaret Buchanan-Smith, eds., Linking Relief and Development, *Bulletin*, Institute of Development Studies, University of Sussex 25, no. 4, 1994; Krishna Kumar, The Nature and Focus of International Assistance for Rebuilding War-Torn Societies, in *Rebuilding Societies after Civil War*, ed. Krishna Kumar (Boulder, CO: Lynne Rienner, 1997), 30 ff.; Ian Smillie, *Relief and Development: The Struggle for Synergy*, Humanitarianism and War Project Occasional Paper 33 (Providence: Brown University, Watson Institute, 1998); Development Assistance Committee of the OECD, *Guidelines on Conflict, Peace and Development Cooperation and DAC Policy Statement*, http://www.oecd.org/dac/htm/pubs/p-cpdc.htm; Nicole Ball, *Making Peace Work: The Role of the International Development Community* (Washington: Overseas Development Council, 1996); and Peter Uvin, *The Influence of Aid in Situations of Violent Conflict*, Paris: Development Assistance Committee of the OECD, 1999.

aid agencies if they are to be effective. And unlike the delivery of relief, they are still highly experimental.

Similarly, they are different from traditional development interventions because they aim at reconstructing social and political institutions in recipient countries, whereas traditional development interventions typically rely on existing social and political structures to deliver their aid and achieve their goals. Their conceptual and organizational place in relation to traditional development work and relief assistance is still a subject of debate.

Their relationship to broader foreign policy goals is also increasingly becoming a topic of discussion. It has been argued (primarily by Department of State officials) that relief and transition assistance, because it can be so highly charged politically and is a potentially important tool of US foreign policy today, should be a more integral part of foreign policymaking, and preferably should be housed in the Department of State. As of this writing, the Department of State was circulating a study on the organization of US bilateral aid for relief and recovery, with one of the most significant options being to relocate the Office of Foreign Disaster Assistance (OFDA), currently housed in USAID, to the Department of State, combining it with the Refugee Program already part of that department. Whereas the Department of State argues that aid for relief and recovery should be part of that organization, USAID argues that, because of the connections to development, relief and recovery assistance should be located in the aid agency. NGOs delivering relief and recovery assistance are generally reluctant to see assistance move even closer to foreign policy decision makers, fearing that the right to humanitarian relief (regardless of the political orientation of the government of the country receiving the aid) to which most of them subscribe would be compromised if foreign policy concerns were given a stronger hold over decisions on such aid.

But here, too, new debates have arisen. Although most humanitarian organizations resist any suggestion that humanitarian relief should be conditional on political considerations, some of them, together with experts on humanitarian assistance, are raising the difficult question: When does humanitarian aid prolong a crisis rather than help relieve the suffering it creates—and, by implication, when should such assistance be terminated, even if a crisis is not over? Aid to relieve starvation in North Korea, governed by a callous and brutal regime (and likely to help prolong the life of that regime), has given particular urgency to this question—although this is not the only case that has raised this issue in recent years.[8]

---

8. Another crisis in which this issue became significant involved the refugee camps for Rwandan Hutus who had fled to the former Zaïre in the aftermath of the genocide in their country. A number of the camps came to be controlled by Hutu militias who had been responsible for the genocide of Tutsis and who were using aid together with threats of violence against the refugees to prevent them from returning to Rwanda. In this case,

These three important issues—the policy and organizational relationship of relief and recovery assistance to development, its relationship to foreign policy, and its negative as well as positive impacts on crisis and human suffering—will without doubt continue into the new century and have an important influence both on US aid for relief and recovery as well as its organizational location.

Political and Economic Transitions

Another purpose that gained prominence in US aid during the 1990s was the support of transitions to free markets and democracy in formerly socialist countries. Twenty-six countries in Eastern Europe and the former Soviet Union have benefited from transition assistance, including Armenia, Azerbaijan, the Czech Republic, Georgia, Hungary, Kazakhstan, Poland, Romania, Russia, the Ukraine, and others. These programs consist primarily of technical assistance and training in such areas as promoting private business (e.g., through privatization and regulatory and legal reform); cleaning up the environment; financing elections; political party and media training; reforming and strengthening a professional, independent judiciary; and supporting a variety of indigenous NGOs. Transition aid was intended to last only a few years. Several bilateral aid programs in Eastern Europe—those for the Czech Republic, Estonia, and Slovenia—have in fact already been phased out. Others, particularly in the poorer countries of Central Asia, are beginning to resemble conventional development programs. Still others, for example, in the countries that are reforming more slowly, such as the Ukraine, may continue and even increase for some time. Most US bilateral aid for economic and political transitions is directed by several regional and country coordinators in the Department of State and implemented by USAID. Some bilateral aid comes from other US government agencies. The United States also provides aid for this purpose through the multilateral development banks, including the World Bank and European Bank for Reconstruction and Development.

Democracy

Both the Bush and Clinton administrations have emphasized the promotion of democracy as a key purpose of US foreign policy. In 1996, for

---

relief was contributing to a prolongation of the refugee crisis and supporting financially those who had committed atrocities in the first place. One major NGO—Medicins sans Frontiers—actually terminated its participation in the relief effort on the grounds that it was prolonging the crisis. For more on the difficult issue of when relief can contribute to disasters rather than relieve them, see Mary B. Anderson and Peter J. Woodrow, *Rising from the Ashes: Development Strategies in Times of Disaster*, Boulder, CO: Westview Press, 1994.

example, the former National Security Advisor, Tony Lake, declared that "our special role in the world is to safeguard and strengthen the community of democracies and open markets. . . ."[9] Promoting democracy is sometimes justified as an end, as an expression of the most sacred of US values, responding to the aspirations of freedom of people throughout the world. Promoting democracy is also explained as a means to an end in that it leads to the realization of other important US values—protection of human rights, religious tolerance, and the rule of law. Additionally, it is justified as strengthening world peace. There is a body of research, cited on occasion by President Clinton, that holds that democracies do not make war on one another and are less prone to internal conflict. Thus, expanding the number of democracies is justified as a means of reducing the probability of violent conflict in the world.[10] It has also been argued that democracy acts as a precondition for development by promoting good governance, including transparency and accountability, on the part of governments. The initiation of rapid growth under authoritarian regimes in Chile, South Korea, Taiwan, and elsewhere suggests that reality is rather more complex.[11]

US foreign aid for this purpose has been used to symbolize US support for opposition forces demanding political reform. (By implication, US engagement has also provided those forces a measure of "insurance" against arrest or assassination.) It has been used as an incentive to pressure governments to adopt political reforms. And it has funded advice on drafting constitutions and laws; the costs of elections; political party training; training for legislators, judges, and journalists; and equipment for government institutions. It has also been used to strengthen NGOs on the theory that civil society organizations operating in the political realm—such as human rights groups and civic education agencies—are essential to preserve democratic practices. Funding for these activities is largely from USAID, but from a number of other agencies as well, including the Department of State, the National Endowment for Democracy, and even the Department of Agriculture.

---

9. Anthony Lake, Laying the Foundation for a New American Century, US Department of State Dispatch 7, no. 18, April 29, 1996.

10. These views are not uncontested. See Henry S. Farber and Joanne Gowa, Polities and Peace; Edward D. Mansfield and Jack Snyder, Democratization and the Danger of War; and David Spiro, The Insignificance of the Liberal Peace—all in *Debating the Democratic Peace*, eds. Michael Brown, Sean Lynn-Junes, and Steven Miller, Cambridge, MA: MIT Press, 1997.

11. For a detailed discussion of the role and impact of aid in promoting democracy, see Thomas Carothers, *Aiding Democracy Abroad*, Washington: Carnegie Endowment for International Peace, 1999.

Other Rationales for US Aid

Two other rationales have been offered to justify US aid that cannot be classified as "purposes," according to the definition offered above, because they do not play a significant role in decisions on where the aid is spent or what sorts of activities it funds. One is using foreign aid to expand US exports and the other is using aid to prevent conflict.

Export Promotion

The expansion of US export markets has never been a primary goal of US foreign aid—that is, determining which countries received aid and how the aid was used.[12] The United States, unlike Japan, France, or Italy, has rarely used its aid to put together "mixed credits" (packages of highly concessional financing combined with the harder terms typical of export credits) to compete for export contracts. At the beginning of the 1990s, there was a move in Congress to direct significantly increased amounts of US bilateral aid to financing infrastructure abroad as a means of enhancing US exports (particularly of the construction industry). However, this move was quashed early in the Clinton administration in a report of an internal US government task force on US foreign aid. This "Wharton Report" (named for Deputy Secretary of State Clifton R. Wharton, Jr., who led the task force) urged that "the United States should maintain strong support for both development assistance and export promotion programs, but they should remain separate. . . ."[13]

Although not a primary purpose of US aid, expanding US exports is often a secondary effect of that aid. US bilateral aid has long been tied to the purchase of US goods and services. The United States expects the multilateral development banks to which it contributes to procure at least as much from the US market as the United States provides in financing. Further, US officials have long claimed that US aid, by promoting

---

12. Although the United States has not often allocated its aid to countries with the primary goal of gaining particular export contracts, it does tie at least 80 percent of its aid to purchases of US goods and services. (See USAID, Why Foreign Aid, http://www.info.usaid. gov.) However, there is an important difference in using aid to compete for export and other commercial advantages abroad and using aid for other purposes but requiring that most of the aid is spent in the United States. This is a subtle but important distinction because it affects basic decisions on who gets the aid and for what purposes.

13. Task Force to Reform A.I.D. and the International Affairs Budget, Revitalizing the A.I.D. and Foreign Assistance in the Post-Cold War Era [also known as the Wharton Report from Deputy Secretary Clifton Wharton, the chair of the task force]. Photocopy. September 1993, vii. This report, requested by the secretary of state and the National Security Council (under Presidential Review Directive 20) was drafted by a task force made up of representatives from a variety of US government agencies with an interest in foreign aid. Although completed and unclassified, the study was never published.

economic reforms and growth in poor countries, has indirectly contributed to the increase in demand for US exports on the part of these countries. This is a plausible argument but a difficult one to demonstrate empirically, given all the factors in addition to US aid that have contributed to growth in poor countries and to their demand for US exports.

Preventing Conflict

Crisis prevention or preventive diplomacy has often been cited in recent years as a central theme of US foreign policy. Foreign aid has been justified on the grounds that one of its effects is to prevent conflict. The root causes of conflict, USAID officials have argued, include poverty, environmental degradation, rapid population growth and urbanization, new diseases, and the absence of democracy.[14] Foreign aid expenditures addressing these "strategic threats," it is argued, will not only help resolve the threats, but will also reduce conflict and support a US diplomacy of conflict prevention.

This rationale for foreign aid, like the previous one, has relatively little influence on the allocation and use of US bilateral aid. It is more an effort to link foreign aid to a central theme of US foreign policy. Although rapid population growth, environmental problems, poverty, or the spread of diseases may exacerbate ethnic or religious tensions within countries or disputes between countries, there is little evidence that intra or interstate conflicts are direct results of such conditions. If this were true, there would be many, many more conflicts than exist today, and some of those that do exist (e.g., those in the Balkans or Northern Ireland) would likely not have erupted.

The Management of US Foreign Aid

There are three principal models for managing US foreign aid today. One is the country programming model used by the multilateral development banks, some international organizations such as UNDP, and USAID. One is what I shall call the rapid response model, used by the OFDA. And one is a foundation model used by the two government foundations (InterAmerican Foundation and African Development Foundation). There is also, of course, the opportunistic model, which simply means that aid agencies or programs provide assistance in response to opportunities or pressures at a particular moment. Most aid agencies

---

14. For one exposition of this argument, see USAID, USAID's Strategies for Sustainable Development, http://www.info.USAID.gov/about/overview.htm.

engage in a degree of opportunistic assistance as a result of political pressures on them or to take advantage of unanticipated occasions to realize their broader goals.

Country programming refers to a set of processes that typically include the aid agency's assessment of the overall economic and social conditions in a recipient country, a strategy for its interventions, the design and implementation of the interventions, and an evaluation of the outcome or impact of the interventions. Country programming was adopted by many aid agencies in the 1960s and 1970s and often combined with a sizable field presence to enable aid agencies to manage their aid interventions in foreign countries. Most of the world's large aid agencies—including the World Bank, USAID, and UNDP—now all have such field missions. These programming processes and field missions are consistent with large aid interventions to promote long-term changes in recipient countries. The World Bank fits into this category, but USAID arguably no longer does. The amount of US bilateral aid in most foreign countries is now relatively small, with the exception of Egypt and a handful of others. The average aid level planned for African countries in 2000, for example, was $20 million, with the largest program ($50 million) planned for Uganda. The average for the 19 countries in Latin America and the Caribbean receiving US bilateral aid in 2000 was just under $20 million. The largest program there was $70 million for Haiti.

US bilateral aid in the past several years has "deconcentrated" for most of the world—that is, the United States has been providing small amounts of aid to a large number of countries worldwide (probably more than 100, according to USAID officials), even though US aid has declined substantially in the past decade. In only a handful of countries—Bosnia-Herzegovina, Egypt, Israel, Jordan, Russia, the Ukraine, and West Bank/Gaza—has US bilateral aid exceeded $100 million. (Not included in these figures is the supplemental aid in 2000 for disaster recovery in Central America and Kosovo.)

Not only do these data show that US aid, for the most part, no longer represents a significant transfer of resources to other countries relative to the size of their economies, but also that where those resource transfers are large, many of them involve relief, peacemaking, or support for transitions—not for traditional long-term development interventions. As USAID has moved away from the size and types of aid interventions it managed in the 1960s through the 1980s, its complicated programming mechanisms and field-based structure have become inappropriate. They are increasingly a poor fit for the smaller amounts of available funding, an increasing proportion of which is allocated to such purposes as peacemaking and disaster response.

In fact, it can be argued that, in significant measure, these programming processes have for some time been a poor fit for what USAID really did. They function on the assumption that the agency sets broad policy directions and strategies, and that the field missions design and implement programs and budgets each year on the basis of their assessment of the needs and opportunities in their respective countries as well as the lessons of past aid interventions. But, the categories of activities for which US bilateral aid is expended are more and more set by Congress and the headquarters in Washington and not USAID's field missions, undercutting the legitimacy of existing programming systems. In short, these systems are badly out of sync with the realities of US bilateral aid and need to be fundamentally recast.

A second model of aid management is "rapid response," in which an aid agency or program has a broad purpose—usually humanitarian relief—and the budget, flexibility, and trained staff to respond to unanticipated crises and opportunities quickly. The OFDA in USAID, which has such a system, is able to get its staff and consultants into the field in response to a crisis within hours to assess needs and organize a quick response. In recent years, OFDA and the Department of Defense often have coordinated effectively to provide relief in humanitarian emergencies, demonstrating that when purposes are clear and programming systems appropriately flexible in different agencies, effective coordination is achievable. The aid management system of the OFDA is an appropriate and effective one.

A third model for managing foreign aid is the foundation model, in which an aid agency makes clear its purpose, substantive areas where it is willing to work, and the standards of performance and accountability it expects in the activities it funds. It then seeks and accepts proposals for funding projects in its focus areas. (These proposals need not come solely from community groups, but could include business enterprises and associations, universities, local or central governments, or other qualified organizations.) Typically, the proposals are conceived and designed by the implementers. If they are acceptable to the foundation, funding is provided and the progress of the activity is monitored. A final report and at times an evaluation is also part of the process.

This approach to aid-giving is far less intrusive, and potentially less staff intensive and organizationally complex than the country programming approach. It should not require a large field presence. It puts more responsibility on the implementers than a country programming system would for designing and managing the aid-funded activity. It can be much more effective for encouraging new and innovative activities, and it is also more amenable to collaborative funding with other aid donors (including NGOs or corporate enterprises) than a country programming approach. A foundation approach to aid management, however, is not so appropriate for large aid transfers to bring about broad social and economic change in recipient countries.

We shall return to these models in the concluding chapters when we focus on the management of US foreign aid in the new century.

The Organization of US Foreign Aid

It is difficult to think of a word other than cluttered to describe the organizational landscape of US foreign aid at the end of the 20th century. There are four bilateral aid agencies, seven multilateral development banks, and nearly 70 international organizations and programs (mainly associated with the United Nations) working in the areas encompassed by the purposes of US aid. A number of these agencies share decision making on individual aid programs, and many run programs similar to those of other agencies. Many of them use their aid to further a mix of the purposes described above, although none of them classifies its expenditure in terms of those purposes. These organizations are listed in table 2.1.

The specific purposes of each of these organizations are described in appendix A. However, several general points can be made here about them. In theory, there is a concept that differentiates these different aid agencies. Bilateral aid agencies and programs—especially in a country with the leadership responsibilities of the United States—tend to be heavily influenced by those responsibilities. Bilateral aid thus becomes a useful tool for such purposes abroad described above because it can be easily controlled and deployed. Aid channeled through the World Bank focuses primarily on development, and because the Bank is multilateral, that aid leverages aid from many other governments that might not be available if the Bank did not exist. Regional development banks can address some of the more sensitive development issues (e.g., policy reforms, social change, or reform of the state) more effectively than the World Bank because of their closer relationships to the governments of their regions and the greater say those governments have in what the regional banks do. International organizations can use their funding to address issues of worldwide concern by calling the attention of governments to those issues, monitoring their evolution, helping member states deal with them, and, where they have the authority, enforcing international norms and rules involving those issues.

The reality of the organizational landscape of foreign aid is much less clear than this ideal. Over the years, many aid organizations have taken on similar tasks, overlapping with others. As we have seen, USAID, the World Bank, UNDP, and others all now have crisis intervention and recovery programs. They all have programs involving "governance" in developing countries. The Bank and the IMF (not considered an aid agency for the purposes of this study) address both problems of economic policy reform. One could go on and on.

The advantage of organizational overlap is that multiple sources of funding can be brought to bear on particular issues. The disadvantages are that organizations that try to do everything often do nothing well. And a multiplicity of organizations dealing with similar issues can lead

Table 2.1 Organizations funded with US foreign aid

Bilateral organizations	Multilateral organizations	International organizations and programs[a]
Agency for International Development	World Bank	United Nations Development Program
Peace Corps	Inter-American Development Bank	UN Children's Fund
InterAmerican Foundation	Asian Development Bank and Fund	International Fund for Agricultural Development
African Development Foundation	African Development Bank and Fund	UN High Commissioner for Refugees
Other US government agencies	European Bank for Reconstruction and Development	World Food Program
	North American Development Bank	UN Population Fund
	Economic Cooperation and Development Bank for the Middle East and North Africa	Food and Agriculture Organization
		Consultative Group on International Agricultural Research
		Inter-American Institute for Cooperation on Agriculture
		World Health Organization
		Pan American Health Organization
		UN Environment Program
		Montreal Protocol Fund
		Global Environment Facility
		Convention on International Trade in Endangered Species of Wild Fauna and Flora
		Organization of American States Development Assistance Program

a. This list includes only those organizations and programs that received $1 million or more from the United States in 1998.

to serious problems of coordination. The organizational landscape of US foreign aid thus presents both a challenge and an opportunity to those rethinking US aid in the new century. We shall return to the topic in the final chapter.

Purposes, Organizations, and Programs: First Cut at a Matrix

How much US aid is provided by these organizations for the six purposes described in this chapter? Two factors make this question difficult to answer accurately. One is that aid agencies do not collect data in the categories of purpose that we have identified. A second is that aid is frequently provided for several purposes, which may be difficult to

**Table 2.2 US foreign aid matrix: Purposes, programs,
organizations, and budget** (fiscal year 1998)

Purpose	Amount (dollars)	Organization	Program
Security or peacemaking	2.4 billion	State Department/USAID	ESF
Development (both traditional and humane interventions)	3.4 billion	USAID, UNDP, MDBs, Peace Corps, InterAmerican Foundation, African Development Foundation, UNICEF, the Treasury, USDA	DA, debt forgiveness Food aid
Humanitarian relief	1.3 billion	USAID, State Department, USDA	DA, State Refugee Fund
Transnational	400 million	USAID, State Department, various international organizations and programs	DA, NADBank
Transitions	1.5 billion	USAID, EBRD, World Bank	SEED/NIS
Democracy	170 million	USAID, State Department, National Endowment for Democracy	DA, ESF
Total	9.2 billion		

Note: ESF = Economic Support Fund; DA = Development Assistance; MDBs = multilateral development banks; EBRD = European Bank for Reconstruction and Development; SEED/NIS = Support for East European Democracy Act and new independent states of the former Soviet Union; USDA = United States Department of Agriculture. The total here differs from that of the DAC, cited earlier, due to the inclusion of aid to Israel, Eastern Europe, and the former Soviet Union.

Sources: USAID, *Congressional Presentation 1999*; US Department of State, Office of the Secretary of State, *Summary and Highlights FY 1999 International Affairs (Function 150) Budget Request*, 2 February 1998.

disentangle. US bilateral aid to Egypt, for example, is provided primarily for security purposes related to peace efforts in the Middle East but is used to promote development in Egypt through funding investment projects and policy reform programs. We shall classify programs insofar as possible according to their primary purpose.

Table 2.2 is a matrix of aid purposes and the organizations whose activities fall primarily within those purposes. A separate column for "program" shows how aid programs fit with the purposes and organizations. The table offers a very rough estimate of the 1998 budgetary commitments associated with the six purposes we have identified above.

Because there is a considerable amount of judgment involved in the data presented in this matrix, I have included in appendix B an explanation of how I arrived at the budget numbers.

Table 2.2 does not include funds spent by domestic US government agencies, because reliable data are not available. But it seems likely that at least another $1 billion could reasonably be added to this chart, largely under the category of transnational issues. Further, it does not include funding from the Department of Defense for its participation in humanitarian relief efforts.

It is worth noting that the Treasury is responsible for managing US participation in the multilateral development banks as well as debt relief programs. Also, funding for PL 480 food aid is located in the Department of Agriculture's budget. However, the input of that agency is minimal in the size, allocation, and use of food aid.

There is no reasonable way of dividing funding for humane concerns and those for traditional development work on the basis of available data. Funding for economic transitions remains relatively large, despite the decreasing number of recipients during the past 5 years, as a number of former socialist countries have made significant progress toward creating free markets and democratic systems or reached the point where they can continue without concessional support. (A significant proportion of this funding—over $200 million—is provided to fund reconstruction in Bosnia.) Finally, for most of these purposes, aid comes from a number of organizations and programs. The table offers a highly simplified picture of a much more complex and overlapping set of organizations and programs for each purpose.

3

The Politics of US Foreign Aid

No comprehensive study of US foreign assistance today and of its probable future can leave out an examination of the politics of foreign aid—the process by which key policy and allocative decisions are made and the influence on those decisions of the Executive Branch bureaucracy, Congress, private groups, foreign governments and international organizations, and public opinion. The purpose of this chapter is to provide that essential political dimension.

Because foreign aid involves the expenditure of sizeable amounts of public resources, policymaking and politics typically occur within the budget and congressional appropriations processes. It is there we shall look to understand the politics of US foreign aid. The budgetary process, involving both the Executive Branch and Congress, has changed little during the past decade. But the political environment has shifted over that time, with the end of the Cold War and pressures to reduce discretionary spending to shrink the budget deficit. The role of various actors in the process also shifted during the 1990s, with Congress and private groups exerting increasing influence over foreign aid programs—except for funding for peacemaking. An examination of the process and the actors in it will elaborate on these observations.

The Budgetary Process and Foreign Aid

Foreign aid policies are often announced by the Executive Branch—for example, on the occasion of a new administration taking office or in response to fundamental changes in the world. But whether those policies

Table 3.1   The budgetary process for foreign aid: USAID

Jan. 2000	March-Sept. 2000	Sept.-Dec. 2000	Feb. 2001	March-Oct. 2001	Oct. 2001
Instructions to field missions to prepare budgets for FY 2002	Budgetary decisions within USAID/ informal negotiations with State Department	Budgetary decisions by OMB and president	Transmission of budget to Congress	Congressional action on budget and appropriations bills	Beginning of FY 2002

Note: OMB = Office of Management and Budget; FY = fiscal year.

are implemented or not is decided primarily in the annual budgetary process, which involves both the Executive Branch and Congress and includes not only proposed overall budget levels but aid allocations by country and purpose.

The budgetary process for foreign aid is a long and complex one, commencing roughly a year and a half before the beginning of the fiscal year in which the budget is spent. Table 3.1 sets out the timeline for this process for USAID in fiscal year 2002.

This process can be even further prolonged when Congress fails to pass a foreign aid appropriations bill before the beginning of the fiscal year. Then there must be a continuing resolution until a final appropriations bill is passed. Under these circumstances, which are not uncommon, the entire budgetary process can take up to 2 years or even longer.

The process begins when foreign aid agencies undertake internal budget reviews (including, at times, informal negotiations with other interested agencies) to produce their budget proposals for the coming fiscal year. These proposals typically include not just the overall levels of aid but detailed information on the amounts intended for particular purposes—for example, family planning—and for particular regions and countries. (US contributions to multilateral development banks and international organizations do not have this degree of detail because the United States does not have control over the country allocation and use of those funds. The levels of these contributions are negotiated periodically with other member states of these organizations and then sent by the administration to Congress in its annual foreign aid budget requests.) Agencies send their budget proposals to the OMB for further review and decision by the president.

Following the president's decisions, there is almost always an appeal from the secretary of state for more bilateral aid. After a final decision (usually involving a small increase over his initial level), the president transmits his entire budget to Congress in February. As with the budgets for many other federal programs, the overall aid budget proposed to Congress will typically have a small increase over the level of the previous year. (Administrations seldom ask for significantly increased aid levels—except to respond to a crisis or major opportunity abroad—realizing that such a request can generate political ridicule or a backlash in Congress. In recent years, the major increases in foreign aid have all come in supplemental requests.) The details of the allocation of aid by organization, and for bilateral aid by country and purpose, are also provided to Congress in a series of "Congressional Presentations" from each bilateral aid agency and by the federal departments responsible for US contributions to multilateral organizations.[1]

Upon receiving the proposed aid budget, Congress begins its deliberations. These first involve decisions by the budget committees on overall spending levels and decisions by the appropriations committees on "caps" (i.e., the maximum amount of appropriations permitted), allocated to each of 13 appropriation subcommittees. The subcommittees in the House of Representatives and Senate responsible for foreign aid are the foreign operations subcommittees.

In theory, a second step in this process would be action by the authorization committees in each house responsible for particular aid programs. These committees—the main ones being the House International Relations Committee and Senate Foreign Relations Committee for bilateral aid and the House and Senate finance committees for multilateral aid—are supposed periodically to reauthorize the expenditure of funds for each aid program by passing authorizing legislation that gives policy direction to the administration. In fact, no overall foreign aid authorization bill has passed Congress and been signed by the president since 1985. Successive Congresses have chosen to waive the requirement for authorization, in part because members typically wish to avoid unnecessary votes on foreign aid. But more important, it has proven extremely difficult to obtain a consensus within Congress on authorizing legislation for foreign aid and an agreement between Congress and the administration on the contents of that legislation. (One effort on the part of Congress to pass such legislation failed for want of administration support in 1991, and an attempt on the part of the administration to get Congress to pass new legislation in 1994 failed for want of support in Congress. An effort led by the Senate Foreign Relations Committee in

---

1. These foreign aid programs are included in what is referred to in budget circles as the "150 Account," from the number given to most foreign affairs spending. However, foreign aid provided by domestic US government agencies, including food aid provided by the Department of Agriculture, is not included in this account. Further, the public concessional funding spent abroad by domestic US government agencies is not examined as foreign aid nor included in foreign aid data. It is, in short, not part of foreign aid politics—at least not yet.

1996 to get a foreign aid authorization bill passed and signed by the president failed when he threatened to veto the legislation.)

The absence of reauthorizations has simplified the politics of foreign aid in Congress by eliminating the authorization process. But it has also shifted policymaking almost entirely to appropriations committees whose primary responsibility is to decide spending levels (and, often, to cut those levels) rather than to determine the policies for which the aid is to be spent. The absence of foreign aid policy debates that are supposed to take place within authorizing committees has also likely contributed to a Congress less informed about foreign aid and one in which creating the consensus needed to pass legislation with fundamental policy or organizational changes may have become more difficult and costly for a future administration wishing to make significant reforms in US aid.

The Appropriations Process

The key process in Congress at present involving the size, allocation, and use of foreign aid is the appropriations process. An appropriations bill must be passed annually if aid agencies are to continue to operate or if US contributions to multilateral agencies are to be made. When Congress is unable to pass a foreign aid bill before the beginning of the fiscal year, it passes a continuing resolution, which usually sets funding at the level of the past year. A continuing resolution can last for days, weeks, or an entire fiscal year. At times, when it proves impossible (because of the press of time or for political reasons) to pass a freestanding foreign aid appropriations bill, these appropriations are included in an omnibus spending bill that covers numerous government programs. And because the foreign aid authorization process has virtually ceased to function in Congress, not only budgetary decisions but also policy decisions—affecting which countries receive US aid and how the aid is spent—have been taken over by appropriations committees.[2]

In making their decisions, the foreign operations subcommittees call hearings on the foreign aid budget, inviting not only administration witnesses but outside experts and advocates to testify. They then "mark up" draft legislation and vote the bill out of the subcommittee. (In recent years, the Senate has only marked up the bill in the full Appropriations Committee, skipping the subcommittee stage.) The bill is voted out of subcommittee and, after another markup, is voted out of the full appropriations committees. It is then debated, amended, and voted on by the full House of Representatives or Senate. The two houses then create a joint House-Senate conference committee to negotiate their differences,

2. Not everything can be done through appropriations bills, however. A fundamental reorientation of the foreign aid program or a reorganization that would require legislation would still have to go through an authorization process.

and both houses then vote on the final bill once more. The completed bill then goes to the president for signature. After the president signs the bill, the administration must figure out how to implement it. (The bill usually has a lower level of aid than requested and numerous earmarks and directives on how and where the funds should be spent.) During the legislative process, extensive informal negotiations typically take place between members of Congress and their staffs and administration officials on what the administration's true priorities are and what it will accept in the bill. Negotiations are also held with important outside interest groups on their wishes and preferences.

In addition to the regular budgetary process, the Executive Branch may also send to Congress budget amendments and supplementals to ask for additional appropriations for unexpected contingencies. In recent years, when Congress was trying to reduce the budget deficit, all such additional requests for funds had to include offsets—reductions in expenditures elsewhere in the overall federal budget to ensure that total expenditures remained under planned ceilings. With the emergence of budget surpluses, pressure to find offsetting reductions elsewhere in the budget have eased (e.g., through additional expenditures being declared emergencies—whether they are or not—that do not require offsets).

This brief description of the key decision-making processes involving foreign aid provides only the bare framework in which budgetary, policy, and allocative decisions are made. Let us now examine in greater detail the actors in this process and how they interact to influence decisions, and how those interactions have changed during the past decade.

Actors and Interactions

We now examine each of the major groups of actors in the politics of foreign aid: The Executive Branch agencies, Congress, private organizations, foreign governments and international organizations, and public opinion.

The Executive Branch

There are five major players in the politics of foreign aid in the Executive Branch: The Department of State, USAID, the Treasury (responsible for multilateral development banks), the OMB, and the White House (including the NSC, the president and at times the vice president, and the first and second ladies).

The Department of State has long been the preeminent Executive Branch player in foreign aid issues. It is the key decision maker for US voluntary contributions to international organizations, including the UNDP, UNICEF, and others. It is the principal actor in decisions on the overall size, country allocation, and—to an increasing extent—use of ESF monies. (ESF, it will be remembered from the previous chapter, is a program of bilateral aid provided primarily for security or political purposes. Much of this aid goes to countries of the Middle East. Its delivery and implementation are managed largely by USAID.) The State Department also participates in decision making on the country allocation and, at times, the use of Development Assistance—the bilateral aid program directed and managed by USAID.

Two trends appear to mark the State Department's engagement in foreign aid issues during much of the past decade. One is the declining relevance of development aid for the State Department's priorities. The other is the increasing efforts by the department to exert greater control over US bilateral aid resources generally.

The department's interest in and advocacy of aid for development—as reflected in testimony, speeches, and attention from senior officials—appears to have diminished considerably during the past decade. For example, in late 1999, an opinion piece by Secretary of State Madeleine Albright urged Congress to increase appropriations for foreign affairs spending by emphasizing the need for the United States to "defuse crises, repel dangers, promote more open economic and political systems and strengthen the rule of law" and to "address urgent humanitarian needs such as child survival, clearing land mines, caring for refugees and slowing the spread of HIV/AIDS."[3] "Development" was never mentioned.

The reasons for this trend are not hard to find. The end of the Cold War reduced US strategic concerns in the developing world, and with it the relevance to foreign policy officials of aid for development. But perhaps more important, the most difficult development problems are concentrated in Sub-Saharan Africa, where the United States has the fewest strategic, political, and economic interests. (There is a broad but still relatively weak constituency for US engagement in Africa, made up primarily of African-American groups and humanitarian organizations. It has thus far been unable to raise significantly the priority of the region in US foreign policy.) Additionally, with considerable economic progress in Asia and Latin America during the past several decades and the increasing and diverse US ties in those regions, foreign aid as a diplomatic tool for US ambassadors—for example, to ensure access to government officials—has become far less useful. (It still, however, remains useful—even essential—for US diplomats in Africa, where there are far fewer trade, investment, and other ties. But Africa remains at the lower end of the list of regional concerns, and so the diplomatic usefulness of development aid

---

3. *The Washington Post*, 9 September 1999.

there does not translate into a major priority for that aid at the senior levels of the State Department.)

A second trend evident in the State Department during the past several years has been an effort to gain greater control over bilateral aid resources. The major tactic in this effort has involved proposals to merge all or part of USAID with the Department of State. The declining relevance of development aid and a view on the part of some senior State officials that more aid resources were needed to give greater influence (both inside and outside the State Department) to US diplomatic initiatives involving transnational issues led Secretary of State Warren Christopher in 1994 to propose a merger of USAID into the State Department. Vice President Gore agreed that the National Performance Review (attached to his office) would undertake a study of the organization of several foreign affairs agencies, including the option of a merger. USAID opposed the idea on the grounds that such a merger would undercut its development mission. The vice president eventually decided against such a merger, but the issue was then taken up by Senator Jesse Helms and others in Congress, who sought to force the administration to implement a merger through legislation and political bargaining. The administration agreed to fold two other small agencies (the Arms Control and Disarmament Agency and US Information Agency) into the State Department but refused to include USAID in that merger.[4]

The issue of a merger between USAID and the Department of State is dormant but not dead as of this writing. It arose again in 1999 with another study, mentioned in the previous chapter, about the organization of US programs and agencies charged with responding to humanitarian emergencies abroad. The contest for control over bilateral aid and, by implication, over the purposes for which that aid is used, will continue in the new century until there is a consensus within the Executive Branch and in Congress on the future directions of US aid.

Having mentioned USAID several times already, let us now turn to it as a political actor in the foreign assistance drama. It is responsible for managing the three major bilateral aid programs—Development Assistance, ESF, and PL 480. It has the policy leadership in Development Assistance and food aid but must negotiate with the Department of State on the country allocation of Development Assistance and, at times, of food aid as well.

The best way to think about USAID's political role is as an advocate, within the Executive Branch, with Congress, private groups, and the

---

4. What was decided was to place the administrator of USAID "under the direct authority and foreign policy guidance of the secretary of state," and to shift several positions in USAID's press office to the State Department. In fact, these changes were insignificant, and USAID continues to operate as a semi-independent agency, much as it did before the issue of merger arose.

public, for maximum levels of aid for development and for maximum flexibility to manage that aid. The implicit price to USAID of support from within the Executive Branch, Congress and a variety of organized interest groups for higher levels of foreign aid, is often the allocation of a portion of its resources to the purposes and activities favored by its supporters. As it has come to depend on private organizations more and more for support of its programs in Congress and even in its dealing with the administration (e.g., on the issue of its survival), USAID has lost much of its management flexibility and control over what it spends its funds on.

But USAID does more than advocate. As a relatively weak government agency (because it does not have cabinet-level status), it typically looks for allies within the bureaucracy. When possible, it will play one agency off against another (or one house of Congress off against the other) to advance its interests. For example, when the NSC is actively engaged in aid issues, USAID will, if feasible, seek its support to resist demands from the Department of State. Since the Carter administration, there have been no senior officers in the NSC with expertise on foreign aid and responsibility for aid and development policies, limiting the opportunities to use this tactic. However, in both the Bush and Clinton administrations, the second and first ladies, respectively, have taken an interest in certain of USAID's programs and at times have acted as quiet supporters of those programs and of the survival of USAID as an organization.

When it cannot find allies to defend its programs, USAID sometimes adopts another tactic: It attempts to withdraw from the political fray by refusing to return telephone calls, avoiding interagency meetings, creating barriers of various kinds to moving forward with proposals from other agencies (e.g., by citing multiple regulations that would prevent implementing such proposals), and being generally difficult and time consuming to deal with. This tactic can work, at least in the short run, when other agencies do not feel strongly about their proposals. It cannot work where a proposal is of high priority and another agency has the willingness and ability to force its adoption.

There are three other bilateral aid agencies: The Peace Corps, the InterAmerican Foundation, and the African Development Foundation. The budgets of these agencies are small enough (the Peace Corps' annual budget is just over $245 million; the budgets of the other two agencies are $5 million and $14 million, respectively) to be barely visible on the foreign aid political screen. One—the Peace Corps—has a strong constituency of former volunteers, including a number of members of Congress. The other two have relied on small groups of supporters—often including influential members of Congress and Hispanic or African-American groups—to survive in periods of budgetary stringency and organizational streamlining. In contrast to the much larger USAID, they are left alone by most of the rest of the Executive Branch (apart from periodic grumblings from OMB). Smallness and persistence can help survival and the avoidance of drastic budget cuts.[5]

The Treasury is responsible for US representation in the multilateral development banks. It is usually the sole player in proposing the annual level of US contributions to those organizations (which are, in turn, based on the levels the United States has negotiated with other member states of the banks). There are occasional conflicts between USAID and the Treasury over the funding levels proposed for bilateral versus multilateral agencies—especially when budgets are tight and trade-offs unavoidable. From time to time, there have also been efforts on the part of USAID to gain control over US policies and representation in the banks, using the argument that those organizations are working on development issues that USAID knows far more about than the Treasury and that therefore responsibility for them in the US government should be in USAID.[6] However, this proposal has never been taken seriously outside of USAID, especially because the Treasury is widely regarded as a far more effective advocate of assistance for these organizations than USAID could be.

Other major actors in the foreign aid drama within the Executive Branch include the Office of Management and Budget, and, as already noted, the National Security Council and the president and vice president. OMB is responsible for overseeing the budgetary aspects of foreign assistance and recommending to the president annual budgets for aid agencies and programs. This role gives OMB a basis on which to influence policies as well as budgets, for the two are usually intertwined. Its entree into policy debates typically arises when there are important issues of efficiency and effectiveness of existing policies or when there are proposals for new policies with budgetary implications. It can exert considerable influence on foreign aid policies when important foreign policy concerns are not in play. (OMB is seldom a match bureaucratically for a determined Department of State and almost never for the National Security Council when high priority aid issues are being decided.) OMB's approach to budget and policy issues is often "the less spent, the better." Indeed, it is probably the only agency in the Executive Branch whose officials are rewarded for cutting budgets rather than increasing them. OMB is also charged with evaluating the management of US government agencies, but it has seldom had significant influence or capacity in this area.

---

5. But not always. The InterAmerican Foundation's support in Congress has eroded since Congressman Dante Fascell retired. Recently, its budget was slashed because of dissatisfaction on the part of key members of Congress with its performance and disapproval of its perceived posture distancing itself from US foreign policy.

6. See, e.g., J. Brian Atwood [USAID administrator], The Future of the US Foreign Assistance Program, Overseas Development Council, 29 June 1999, http://www.odc.org.commentary.

Finally, there is the White House—the president, vice president, and NSC—which can trump all the other players when they become engaged in a foreign aid issue. They can also be influenced by the other players, who will, if possible, seek them out as allies.

Few presidents during the past several decades have had much ongoing interest in foreign aid. In contrast to Presidents Kennedy, Johnson, and Nixon, they have made few speeches on the subject or created few blue ribbon committees to study foreign aid issues and make recommendations for overall program and policy changes. The overall diminishing relevance of foreign aid to the high priorities of US foreign policy partly explains this phenomenon. The view on the part of most presidential political advisors that—given the perceived public hostility to foreign aid—paying attention to aid will carry political costs for their bosses, has also led to the diminished importance of foreign aid on the national political agenda.

Presidents do, of course, get interested in aid to help with specific international problems—for example, when there is a sudden crisis or major change in the world for which aid is a useful tool of US policies. A presidential trip abroad can also generate pressures for deliverables in the form of aid commitments, as we have seen in chapter 3. Few vice presidents have shown much interest in aid issues—except Vice President Gore, whose commitment in particular to environmental preservation led to increases in foreign aid for that purpose for several years.

Two further points need to be made regarding the actors on foreign aid within the Executive Branch. First is the "dog that didn't bark" point. In the case of the United States—in contrast to a number of other aid-giving governments—the Department of Commerce, the Export-Import Bank, and other agencies engaged in promoting US trade and investment abroad play almost no role in policy and allocative decisions involving foreign aid. There are several reasons for this. One is that, in the past, the use of foreign aid for diplomatic purposes limited its use for commercial purposes as well. US aid diplomacy that attempted to advance US political interests by expanding US business in Latin America, Africa, and Asia would have been highly suspect and controversial—even more than it was already, simply coming from a great power—and could have led to its rejection by governments under pressure from the left in their countries. In effect, the involvement of the Department of State in influencing foreign aid has helped keep the Commerce Department and other commercially oriented US government agencies out. A second factor that left commercially oriented US government agencies out of decisions on where US aid is spent or how it is used was that US aid was already tied largely to the purchase of US goods and services. The fact that more than 80 percent of US aid is spent in the United States has provided the State Department and USAID with the argument that the US economy and, by implication, US businesses are already benefiting from foreign aid.

A final reason for the limited influence of commercially oriented US government agencies on foreign aid decisions is the relatively small amount of funding provided to most countries—in the range of $10 million to $40 million per year. These are not large amounts from the point of view of major US corporations, and so the potential commercial benefits of trying to influence aid are hardly worth the effort.

The second point in this section on Executive Branch players in the foreign aid game involves the many US government agencies, apart from those specialized in foreign affairs issues, that have initiated their own programs of external assistance during the past decade. They often effectively advocate with USAID to channel its aid monies through them to support their programs abroad in health, labor, transportation, and other activities. A proportion (we do not have data on how much) of USAID's monies, especially in Eastern Europe and the former Soviet Union, continues to be channeled through other US government agencies for a variety of activities.[7]

Congress

The Congress acts primarily by passing legislation. In the case of foreign aid, the key legislative act, as we have already noted, is appropriating funding for assistance programs. And, it is generally understood, the tasks of chairs of the foreign operations subcommittees and their staffs are to craft a foreign aid bill and manage the legislative process so that the bill is eventually passed by Congress and signed by the president. A failure to pass an appropriations bill by the beginning of the fiscal year will lead to a shutdown of government agencies (as in late 1995). Such a shutdown obviously disrupts programs and the personal lives of the employees affected. It is also generally seen as a failure of political leadership in Congress, and so members and, particularly appropriations subcommittee chairs, do their best to get a funding bill passed—if not a freestanding bill, then spending authorities for foreign aid within an omnibus appropriations bill (as in 1997), or as a continuing resolution, which will usually permit the expenditure of funds at the level of the previous fiscal year.

What does it take to get a foreign aid appropriations bill passed? The short answer, of course, is an adequate number of votes. And what does it take to get an adequate number of votes? It takes two things. One is

---

7. USAID's Congressional Presentation for fiscal year 2000 mentions that in Russia, its funds supported activities by the Environmental Protection Agency, Health and Human Services, the Departments of Energy, Agriculture, Commerce, and Justice, the US Forest Service, the Treasury, and the Peace Corps. See http://www.usaid.gov.

arguments justifying the overall purposes of aid that are sufficiently persuasive to garner votes. The other is specific programs and policies within the bill that a coalition of members find attractive enough from the point of view of their own interests and preferences to support. These two components are shaped in a political environment that also has a major influence on the voting behavior of members of Congress. Let us examine in more detail these factors and the role of the political environment in influencing foreign aid legislation.

The major issues of the day affect the congressional politics of any number of government programs. But this is particularly true of foreign aid, for two reasons. First, it is a set of programs with a relatively weak domestic political constituency and thus is particularly vulnerable to the prevailing political winds. The influence of the general political environment was very evident in the sharp cuts in foreign aid made both by Democratic and Republican Congresses in the mid-1990s, reflecting the unhappiness of their constituents during an economic recession and their own efforts to trim large budget deficits. The antigovernment ideological fervor of the Republican Congress that took power in 1995 also contributed to the deep cuts in aid that year, as well as efforts to eliminate USAID and shift its programs into the Department of State.

Second, foreign aid is a tool of US foreign policy, so when there are controversial issues involving US foreign policy, foreign aid legislation becomes a lightning rod for criticism. Such controversies can generate sharp cuts in aid levels, legislative restrictions, and outright defeat of aid bills. This was the case in the early 1970s during the war in Indochina, when a Democratic Congress refused to pass a foreign aid authorization bill to protest the Nixon administration's policies in Vietnam. This was also the case in the 1980s, when a Democratic Congress became increasingly unhappy with the Reagan administration's policies in Central America. And for several decades, foreign aid has been a focus of debate between pro-life and pro-choice members about abortion (because foreign aid funds family planning programs abroad). As one member of the House remarked, foreign aid "can pass if it has no single-issue red flags and if it's supported by the president."[8]

Another element in the political environment involves political parties. It is worth asking here whether the political party in power in Congress makes a difference in foreign aid appropriations. The short answer is not much, especially after the Cold War. As a general matter, Democrats have tended to be more supportive of foreign economic assistance (and resistant to foreign military assistance), while Republicans have been more critical of foreign economic aid and more supportive of military aid abroad. Further, many share the view that Republicans support aid

---

8. The comment was by James Leach (R-Iowa), cited in *Congressional Quarterly Almanac* 47, 1991, 478.

to help promote US economic interests abroad while Democrats are more favorable toward foreign aid that helps the poor.

In fact, the ideological differences between the parties are only the most general guide to their policy preferences and votes on foreign aid. Democrats did cut military aid levels proposed by the Bush administration and increased aid for development several years running. But Republicans, once they gained control of Congress in 1995, did not do the reverse. Rather, since then they have forced the Clinton administration to put more aid into activities related to helping children and have shown no interest in pushing aid into greater support for US commercial interests abroad.[9]

Further, just because the same party controls Congress and the Executive Branch does not mean that foreign aid programs proposed by the latter are strongly supported by the former. One of the deepest cuts in recent times in foreign aid was taken by a Democratic-controlled Congress in the early years of the Clinton administration.

Key factors influencing votes by members of Congress on foreign aid are ideas (i.e., rationales) and interests. The purposes of foreign aid, used by the Executive Branch to justify aid programs, are an important element in the politics of aid in Congress. The two broad purposes of limiting the expansion of Soviet influence and promoting development in poor countries long provided a basis for both liberal and many conservative members to support (or at least not actively oppose) aid appropriations. The disappearance of the security rationale and the weakening of the development rationale since the early 1990s—without the Executive Branch being able to offer compelling substitutes—has had two results. First, the weakened rationale for foreign economic assistance has forced the aid program to rely heavily on a coalition of interests for its passage, and these multiple interests are reflected in the number of earmarks and directives now in the program and reduced flexibility on the part of the administration in managing bilateral aid. Second, a coalition of interests may support passage of appropriations bills if members favoring those interests are numerous and in positions of influence in Congress. But if a large number of newly elected members arrive who have little knowledge of foreign aid, are highly skeptical of its value and rationales, and have no ties to groups supporting it, the aid program can become very vulnerable to attack and deep cuts—as it proved to be in 1995.

The loss of compelling security and development rationales for foreign aid has also led Congress to adopt what has become in effect a

---

9. Ironically, there was a move in the Democratic-controlled Senate at the beginning of the 1990s—led by Democratic Senators Lloyd Benson, Robert Byrd, David Boren, and Max Baucus—to allocate large amounts of US foreign aid for large infrastructure projects abroad that would be implemented by the US construction industry. This move was finally quashed by the Clinton administration, as noted earlier.

Table 3.2   Child survival and disease programs as part of total Development Assistance (millions of US dollars)

	1995	1996	1997	1998	1999	2000
Child survival and disease	571	567	600	650	700	715
Total DA	2,111	1,729	1,733	2,024	1,895	1,923

Note: About $100 million of the child survival funds are earmarked each year for UNICEF.

Source: Congressional Research Service, annual analyses of Foreign Operations Appropriations, various years.

substitute, if unarticulated, rationale—helping disadvantaged children and other groups abroad (which appeals to the humanitarian values of the US public) and addressing the spread of several major diseases, including HIV/AIDS and tuberculosis. Table 3.2 shows the trend in Development Assistance earmarked for child survival and disease-related activities abroad. (The funds allocated to disease average about $150 million to $200 million per year.) In each of these years, the allocations for this purpose by Congress exceeded the administration's request, even when it cut other components of that request.

What sorts of interests, then, motivate members of Congress to vote for foreign aid? Some may have to do with the make up of their constituencies: Members with large numbers of constituents who actively support aid for particular countries or purposes will have a reason to vote for foreign aid. Undoubtedly, the most active and effective constituents for foreign aid (as we shall see in more detail below) are those concerned about the well-being of Israel. But African-Americans, Armenian-Americans, Greek-Americans, church groups, environmentalists, and others also attempt to influence members of Congress to support foreign aid (and often press for earmarks and directives for their particular program preferences).

Members of Congress (and their staffs) often have personal preferences for particular types of aid programs, regardless of whether or not they have sizable numbers of constituents who also support such programs. The support for child survival on the part of many members of Congress, mentioned above, is one example.

Chairs of the foreign operations subcommittees in the House and Senate often add earmarks or directives benefiting particular groups in their own constituencies. They see such earmarks as a form of "seignorage"—a benefit for them in their districts for managing the passage of a sometimes unpopular aid bill. On occasion, members will vote for foreign aid because another member they trust urges them to do so. However, the phenomenon of major figures in the House or Senate—such as a Hubert Humphrey or Jacob Javits in the Senate in the 1970s—being able, on the basis of their own status and reputation, to lead members to vote for foreign aid appears to be a thing of the past. There are few members with the prestige of a Humphrey or Javits and even fewer who are willing to use their influence on foreign aid issues. Members may also vote for foreign aid primarily on the basis of their status or prestige because the president asks them to do so or to vote against legislation because the president threatens a veto. In recent years, the president has lobbied Congress on specific aid issues—on levels for certain programs (e.g., Bosnia or the Wye River Agreement), on organizational issues (which are usually the prerogative of the Executive Branch), and on policies involving family planning and abortion. But for US presidents at the end of the 20th and beginning of the 21st centuries, foreign aid as a whole was not often an issue on which they were willing to spend much personal or political capital with members of Congress.

Members of Congress, wary of the perceived skepticism or hostility of many of their constituents toward foreign aid (especially in times of economic stress at home) also look for "cover" for voting for aid. That cover often takes the form of significant cuts in overall aid programs below the level of the previous year, below the administration's request, or often in the form of an across-the-board cut during floor debates on foreign aid. (One member introduced for years an across-the-board cut—often of only 1 percent—in floor debates in the House of Representatives. The cut was accepted—even, one suspects, arranged in advance by the subcommittee chair managing the bill—during those years in the early 1990s when there was a recession.[10]) These kinds of cuts permit members to claim to their constituents that although they voted for foreign aid, they supported cutting overall aid levels.

What generalizations can we draw from these elements in the congressional politics of foreign aid and from congressional actions in recent years involving foreign aid? First, the political environment matters a lot. When there are economic stresses at home, foreign aid will be vulnerable to cuts. When there are highly controversial foreign policy issues, especially if foreign aid is an element in those issues, foreign aid generally will be vulnerable to attack and cuts.

Second, as long as a compelling rationale for foreign aid is lacking, passage of foreign aid bills will have to rely more on the politics of interests than of ideas and on the preferences of key members of Congress. And although this approach will work when there is continuity of members in Congress who have an interest-based reason for supporting aid,[11] it can make foreign aid both less flexible as a foreign policy tool

---

10. For accounts of these cuts and other details of congressional action, see *Congressional Quarterly*'s reporting on foreign aid.

11. I include here interests based on personal beliefs or preferences as well as interests associated with a member's constituency.

and more vulnerable to attack when there is a major change of congressional leadership or an influx of new members of Congress who do not see a compelling rationale for voting for aid. This is, in part, what happened in Congress in 1995.

Private Groups

It is often said by commentators on the politics of foreign aid that such aid has no constituency within the United States. That is wrong. It does have a complex and growing constituency, though still a relatively weak one overall. The various private organizations that make up the constituency for foreign aid can be grouped into four categories—those supporting aid to particular foreign countries, regions, or ethnic groups; those supporting aid for particular purposes, such as family planning or preserving the environment; those supporting aid in general; and think tanks, which often advocate particular aid policies as well as frame and inform debates on aid. The strongest elements in this constituency include the organizations supporting aid for particular countries (above all for Israel) and those supporting aid for specific types of activities. The third and fourth of these categories are the least influential.

It is not surprising that organizations of Americans supporting aid for particular countries or regions are numerous and active: The United States is made up of many immigrants or their descendants, who often maintain an affinity for or have strong ties of sympathy to their places of origin. However, only a few of these types of organizations play a significant role in the politics of foreign aid. Without doubt, the most effective of them is the American Israel Public Affairs Committee (AIPAC), widely regarded as the second most influential and effective lobbying organization on any issue, foreign or domestic, in the United States.[12] AIPAC has a large grassroots network, with 55,000 members, located throughout the country. Many of these members are leaders in their communities (and therefore can often reach members of Congress quickly when they want to) and are strongly committed to the mission of AIPAC—"to lobby Congress about legislation that strengthens the relationship between the United States and Israel."[13] AIPAC makes sure that each member of Congress is contacted at least once a year by one of its members on an issue of importance. There are many more contacts with members of Congress

---

12. AIPAC has been judged in several surveys of members of Congress and administration officials as the second most effective lobbyist group in the United States, after the much larger and better funded AARP (American Association of Retired Persons). See Jeffrey H. Birnbaum, Washington's Power 25, *Fortune*, 8 December 1997, 144-52. See also Susan Rees, *Effective Non-profit Advocacy*, Aspen Institute, Washington, 1998, http://www.aspeninst.org/dir/polpro/NSRF/ENPA.

13. From AIPAC's mission statement on its Web site, http://www.aipac.org.

who play a key role in shaping aid and other legislation affecting Israel. And although AIPAC does not provide campaign financing, its membership (which does contribute significantly to political campaigns) is often well aware of which members of Congress have been supportive of aid to Israel and which have not. In short, AIPAC has an organization and an influential and active grassroots membership that gives it exceptional clout in Congress and with the administration on foreign aid. Its support of foreign aid appropriations generally (not only the funds for Israel) is widely regarded as crucial to the passage of that legislation annually.

Other organizations supporting aid for particular foreign countries include those favoring Armenia and Greece. Various groups of African-Americans have been supporters of US aid to Sub-Saharan Africa as well.

Organizations supporting aid for particular purposes number in the several hundreds, at least. InterAction (the umbrella organization for NGOs working on relief and development issues) has 160 members, and this membership far from exhausts the field. The better-known groups in this category include environmental organizations (e.g., Nature Conservancy, World Wide Fund for Nature), family planning organizations (e.g., Population Council and Population International), the many organizations that work on problems of relief (e.g., Save the Children), organizations that support micro-enterprise lending (e.g., FINCA or RESULTS), the land grant and other universities that have favored aid for agricultural research and development, community service organizations (e.g., Kiawanis and Rotary International) that support aid funding for international health campaigns (e.g., the eradication of polio), and alliances of organizations—such as those advocating debt relief for poor countries and those supporting international programs to benefit children. Also in this category is the labor movement, represented by the AFL-CIO, which tends to lobby (more with the administration than Congress) for funding for its Center for International Labor Solidarity, and the farmers—who were active supporters of food aid in the past but have tended to lose interest in food aid as US agricultural surpluses have declined.

This category of organizations is the largest and fastest growing element in the private constituency for foreign aid. It tends, however, to be fragmented, with individual organizations or alliances focusing on particular types of aid-funded activities, rather than the broader issues of foreign aid. A number of these types of organizations lobby not only for aid for their preferred activities but for congressional earmarks or directives requiring USAID to fund those activities.

A third category of organizations includes those that support foreign aid in general, usually as a reflection of US values of helping the least advantaged. Faith-based organizations fall into this category. Alliances and coalitions of organizations in the previous category, plus others with a periodic interest in foreign aid, also fall into this category—although such alliances tend to be temporary. They are typically formed to address a serious threat to foreign aid—as in the mid-1990s, after several years of deep cuts in aid—and then tend to dissolve after the threat is passed. This tends to be the smallest and, at most times, the least influential group in the aid coalition.

What is striking about the constituency for foreign aid is that most of it supports a variety of humanitarian-oriented activities or help for particular countries. There is almost no continuous coalition supporting foreign aid for all of the purposes described in the previous chapter, and there is almost no coalition supporting aid for development per se.

Think tanks involved with development issues are relatively few, and their influence appears to be limited. The Overseas Development Council has been active in foreign aid issues in the past, but its efforts and influence have diminished in recent years. No other Washington-based think tank has foreign aid as a significant or continuous part of its research agenda. Universities used to do a considerable amount of research on foreign aid and development issues and contributed to policy debates in the past, but their role has also diminished with cuts in aid funding and fewer opportunities for their graduates to work in the field of development. Some universities still produce technical studies of development aid—usually funded by USAID, the World Bank, or other aid agencies. The Harvard Institute for International Development was one such entity until it was dissolved in June 2000. But the impact of these three institutions on policy debates has been limited during the past several decades. (This contrasts with the situation in the United Kingdom, where several universities and think tanks—including the Overseas Development Institute and the University of Sussex—continue to play an influential role in the discourse on aid and development.)

How do these various groups and alliances influence foreign aid? They lobby administration officials, when possible, and members of Congress and their staffs on foreign aid policies and legislation. Finding influential allies within the Executive Branch or in Congress is an important tactic. They testify before Congress. They attempt to inform the public and mobilize public pressure (e.g., through letter-writing campaigns to members of Congress), and they call the attention of the media to their issues through public events (concerts, demonstrations, etc.) and through meetings with journalists and editorial writers. Some of these organizations can punish members of Congress who oppose their views through adverse publicity or through influencing campaign contributions of their members. And when they can, they will horse-trade with other organizations, members of Congress, and Executive Branch officials, supporting them on other issues in exchange for support on the aid issue they believe important. All of these tactics are a familiar part of interest-group politics in America. The difference on foreign aid is that the private players tend to be less experienced and far less well funded than many of their domestically oriented counterparts, and few of them have issues of high salience ("drop-dead issues") for their members. Even with informed and supportive Americans, issues involving foreign aid are typically one among many issues on their agendas.

Foreign Governments and International Organizations

Foreign governments and international organizations are in theory not supposed to be players in the US political process. But, of course, they are. Foreign governments often hire prominent lawyers, public relations firms, and lobbyists to advise them and represent their interests in Washington. Lobbyists for foreign governments do not appear to wield significant influence on foreign aid issues. However, if foreign governments can find sizable groups of Americans or key individuals in positions of political power who share their goals and are willing to organize and act politically, they can work together to bring considerable influence to bear in the politics of foreign aid. For most foreign governments, however, this is not an option.

International organizations also have their representatives in Washington (who almost always are US citizens, and often former members of Congress or staffers to key members), including, for example, WHO, UNDP, and the International Fund for Agricultural Development. Although these representatives are supposed to provide information to Americans on their organizations and keep their headquarters informed of what happens in Washington, they have been known to urge their agencies' funding preferences on US officials and members and staffers in Congress—often with some success.

Public Opinion

The US public appears to be both supportive and skeptical of foreign aid. Polls show that a majority of Americans support aid to the needy abroad. Many also believe that the United States is spending too much money on foreign aid and would support lower levels. Interestingly, there is a widespread misperception of how much foreign aid the United States actually provides—with polls showing that a majority thinks the United States spends about 15 percent of the federal budget on aid and believe that 5 percent of the budget for foreign aid would be more appropriate.[14] In reality, the amount spent on foreign aid is less than 1 percent of the federal budget, suggesting that there may be latent support for considerably higher levels of aid.

---

14. Steven Kull and I. M. Destler, *Misreading the Public: The Myth of a New Isolationism* (Washington: Brookings Institution, 1999).

At the same time, many members of Congress often prove reluctant to vote for foreign aid, and presidents are typically adverse to making speeches in its favor—suggesting that they perceive a public skeptical or hostile to aid. What do these mixed messages tell us about the role of public opinion in the politics of foreign aid?

Steven Kull and I. M. Destler,[15] in their book, *Misreading the Public: The Myth of the New Isolationism*, found that 80 percent of the US public support the United States sharing its wealth with those in the world in great need. (Only 8 percent of the public wanted to eliminate foreign aid entirely.) However, this support was often lukewarm. Polls show that three-quarters of Americans believe that the United States spends too much on aid, and more than 80 percent felt that much of the aid was wasted or did not get to the people who needed it.

Those believing that too much money was spent on foreign aid were typically misinformed, greatly overestimating just how much of the federal budget goes for foreign aid—as the poll referred to above showed. This exaggerated view of the size of US aid reflects the fact that the US public normally pays little attention to it. Except when there are prominent issues of humanitarian suffering abroad, the public tends to be passive and permissive on issues of aid rather than an active player in aid politics. It appears that the US public reacts to issues involving foreign aid according to the optic through which the aid is presented. If it is a question of helping the needy abroad or an issue of the United States retaining its leadership in the world, public opinion, as reflected in numerous polls, tends to be supportive of aid. However, if issues of foreign aid are seen through the optic of a tradeoff with resources available for addressing domestic problems (especially in times of economic stress), or "welfare for foreigners" or of an inefficient use of the taxpayers' resources, the public is far more critical of foreign aid. Members of Congress wary of being identified with foreign aid may be reacting to the possibility that their support for foreign aid will be presented to their constituents by their critics through a wasteful welfare optic rather than a humanitarian one.

Conclusion

What does this chapter indicate about the political future of US foreign aid? First of all, the constituency for foreign aid is shifting. The Executive Branch remains a major advocate for aid for peacemaking, global issues, democracy, and humanitarian relief. Congress, reflecting the preferences of its members (based in part on what they believe their constituents will

---

15. For a detailed answer to this question, based on extensive polling, see Kull and Destler, Ibid.

support), has elevated programs to help children to a high priority. Private organizations remain key advocates of aid for particular countries and are especially effective on aid for Israel (and its neighbors) and for a variety of activities, involving humanitarian purposes or what we in the previous chapter called global issues. What is almost absent from this constituency is support for development. The administration as a whole has diminished interest in this purpose since the end of the Cold War, and private organizations—because of the fragmented nature of their own activities and interests—are seldom effective advocates of aid for development or for foreign aid as a whole.

However, another look at the findings of this and the previous two chapters suggests that the elements of a new policy paradigm may in fact already exist—albeit unrecognized and unarticulated. The old security purpose has become increasingly a peacemaking purpose—part of a growing focus of US foreign policy generally and one that is important to the administration. The old development purpose has been in part transformed by Congress into a concern for child survival and other humane interventions. Like the old foreign aid policy paradigm, one of these purposes is related to broader US interests and foreign policy goals; the other is related to US values and a concern for helping the least advantaged abroad better their lives. Added to these elements in a new paradigm is a third purpose primarily related to US interests, supported both by the administration and Congress—addressing transnational issues. A fourth, value-driven purpose is the willingness, as in the past, of the American people to respond generously to humanitarian emergencies abroad. These four purposes could become the basis for a policy paradigm that would carry US foreign aid both conceptually and politically into the new century.

4

US Foreign Aid in the Probable World of the 21st Century

To answer the question we posed in the introduction—how should the United States use its concessional resources to promote its interests and values in the new century?—we first need to examine the significant trends, challenges, and opportunities that will define the world in the new century and may require concessional public resources to address. That is the task of this chapter. The final chapter will draw the various themes of this and previous chapters together to propose a vision for US foreign aid in the new century.

The Probable World of the New Century

It is assumed here that the United States will remain the predominant military and economic power in the first quarter of the 21st century and perhaps beyond, and that no other state or group of states will threaten the survival of the United States or the well-being of its population. It is further assumed that the world economy will continue to integrate and expand (though not without occasional setbacks or interruptions). Non-state actors—corporations, NGOs, and international agencies—will play an increasingly influential political role in a world that is more open and liberal politically, and more connected electronically, than at any time in human history.

The United States will neither retreat into isolationism nor become the world's police officer in the new century but will expand its economic interests across the globe and remain politically engaged worldwide. Where it assumes leadership will depend on the nature of challenges beyond US borders, the policy preferences of successive administrations, and the capacity of those administrations to manage increasing political participation by domestic groups in foreign policy issues. Finally, in a world where threats to US survival are minimal, where information is widely available in real time to Americans on events abroad, and where domestic political groups demand a louder voice in US foreign policies, values shared by significant numbers of Americans may well claim a more prominent role in US foreign policy than they have in the past.

These assumptions represent a reasonable projection of current trends in the coming century. However, the world has been in a state of considerable political, economic, and technological change during the past decade, producing unexpected events like the Asian financial crisis, the outbreak of cholera in South America, the eruption of war in Central Africa, and the rapid spread of the Internet. Such changes—including unanticipated technological breakthroughs as well as recessions, economic crises, political turmoil in major countries such as Russia, and major environmental or health threats—could well interrupt or overturn these projections. A widespread domestic backlash to increasing US engagement in the world—for example, related to the adverse effects of globalization or significant failures at peacemaking abroad—could also change the domestic political environment of US foreign policy in the future in ways that are difficult to foresee. In short, unanticipated events could take on more prominence in the new century than they had in the latter half of the last one.

Three Major Trends

Three prominent trends, which are now apparent, are likely to continue in the new century and pose important challenges to the United States. Each has implications—direct or indirect—for the future of US aid. One involves conflicts within and among states. A second involves the increasing prominence of certain transnational issues. A third involves the economic and political impacts of globalization.

Conflict

The end of the Cold War has not meant the end of armed violence in the world. As of 1998, there were 27 conflicts in 26 locations, according to the Swedish International Peace Research Institute (SIPRI),[1] involving the following countries[2]:

---

1. SIPRI defines conflict as prolonged combat between military forces of governments or organized groups in which at least 1,000 people incurred battle-related deaths.

2. See Margareta Sollenberg and Peter Wallensteen, Major Armed Conflicts, in *SIPRI Yearbook 1998: Armaments, Disarmament and International Security*, Stockholm, table 1A, 26-30.

- Afghanistan
- Algeria
- Angola
- Burundi
- Cambodia
- Colombia
- Democratic Republic of the Congo
- Eritrea-Ethiopia
- Guinea-Bissau
- India (two conflicts)
- India-Pakistan
- Indonesia
- Iran
- Iraq
- Israel
- Myanmar
- Peru
- The Philippines
- Rwanda
- Sierra Leone
- Sri Lanka
- Sudan
- Turkey
- Uganda
- Yugoslavia

This snapshot of conflicts in 1998 might appear to substantiate some of the predictions of spreading chaos throughout the world that have appeared in print or in statements of administration officials in recent years—for example, the widely read essay The Coming Anarchy by Robert Kaplan,[3] which predicted a dire future of deepening disorder, especially in the poorer regions of the globe. This would be a mistake. Data on world conflicts after 1987 show a decline in the number of armed conflicts during the past decade, from 37 in 1989 to 27 in 1998.[4]

However, the data also tell us that the nature of conflict has shifted. In 1998, all but 2 of the 27 conflicts in the world were civil conflicts— violence by armed groups within states rather than violence between states. These conflicts tended to be prolonged, drew in other countries, became highly destructive of life and property, and frequently generated large flows of refugees, and internally displaced people. Displaced people and refugees, typically without resources, require large expenditures of funds by their host countries and the international community to provide them with food, shelter, medicine, and other needs. Table 4.1 shows recent annual estimates of displaced people and refugees.

What are the prospects for conflict in the new century? The tensions between India and Pakistan over Kashmir could, if not controlled, erupt in a dangerous war, which could well include nuclear weapons. The war between Ethiopia and Eritrea, which now appears to have ended,

---

3. See Robert Kaplan, The Coming Anarchy, *Atlantic Monthly*, February, 1994, 44-76.

4. SIPRI, op. cit., 17.

Table 4.1 Refugees and relief, 1991-98 (millions)

	1991	1992	1993	1994	1995	1996	1997	1998
People of concern[a]	17.0	19.0	23.0	27.4	27.4	26.1	22.7	22.4

a. People of concern include refugees, former refugees who have returned to their home countries, internally displaced people, and others, including war victims. The data do not include Palestinian refugees. Refugees and displaced people may result from natural disasters, but the bulk of them are victims of conflicts.

Sources: persons of concern: UN High Commissioner for Refugees, from US Department of State, *Congressional Budget Presentation FY 1999 and FY 2000* (Washington: US Government Printing Office).

was also a dispute over territory. Wars in central Africa—not over land but over political allegiances, fueled by competition for control over natural resources—continue despite periodic ceasefires and promises of peace among the governments involved. Tensions among Middle Eastern countries appear under control at the time of this writing, but the region has long been one of surprises.

Despite these and other flashpoints in world politics at the beginning of a new century, one of the striking things about conflict in the past half-century is the decrease in the number of interstate conflicts over land and resources. It may be that the norms of behavior among states, the institutions such as the United Nations working for peace, the intensifying network of economic and other relationships—and possibly even the spread of democracy—have combined to discourage interstate conflict and make many of the conflicts that do threaten regional peace more manageable. If this interpretation is correct, the probable world of the 21st century will suffer from few interstate conflicts—albeit potentially quite deadly ones involving weapons of mass destruction.

A look at the factors leading to intrastate conflict, however, produces a far less optimistic picture of the future. Civil conflicts have been concentrated in countries or regions where several of the following elements are present—where societies are poorly integrated—that is, where ethnic, religious or regional identities are stronger than national identities; where political leaders have exploited such differences for political gain—either by playing on social identities or by favoring, excluding, or repressing particular groups; where governments are too weak to prevent the formation and arming of insurgent domestic groups (and external support for those groups); and where there are few effective regional security arrangements (involving regional or international organizations or influential external powers) that can mediate emerging conflicts before they erupt into full-scale violence. One other element appears to be present in some of today's civil conflicts—a history of recent armed violence, the political and social aftereffects of which have not been overcome. The conflicts in Cambodia and Angola and the genocide in Rwanda and massacres in Burundi during the 1990s were direct consequences of earlier armed violence—after which warring parties never fully laid down their arms nor addressed the problems that fed the violence in the first place or the abuses that took place during the violence.

Not only weak and incompetent states but new states are vulnerable to civil violence. Not surprisingly, many civil conflicts at the end of the 21st century were in countries created in the breakup of empires—in the Balkans after the breakup of Yugoslavia and, above all, in Africa, as a delayed reaction to the end of European colonialism and the end of the Cold War. It remains to be seen whether the new states emerging out of the breakup of the Soviet Union will also fall victim to civil disorder. Some, such as Tajikistan in Central Asia, and others, such as Georgia, Armenia, and Azerbaijan in the Caucasus, already have experienced sporadic civil violence. A breakup of Indonesia, feared by many as of this writing, could also produce violence within and among the new states formed out of that country. The conditions giving rise to civil conflict in Africa, the Balkans, and elsewhere do not appear likely to abate in the near future, and therefore such conflicts will be part of the probable world of the early 21st century.

Not only does the new century appear to promise a continuing number of civil conflicts that will require external intervention for making peace and providing humanitarian relief, but also what appears to be increasing international tolerance and support for external military and humanitarian interventions to stop serious human rights abuses—as in Iraq and Kosovo—seems likely to result in an expanded definition and mandate for peacemaking and humanitarian relief in the 21st century. The United States, as the world's leading power, will at times want to assume responsibility for peacemaking if other alternatives are lacking. Foreign aid will be an important component of any peacemaking policy, acting as it has in the past as an inducement to the warring parties to stop fighting and as a resource to help them to recover. The challenge for future US administrations will be to define the extent and limits of their policies of peacemaking. This policy will, in turn, define the need for aid for this purpose.

Transnational Problems

We noted in chapter 3 that addressing transnational problems of environment, health, and scarcities of key resources had begun to emerge as a distinct purpose of US aid during the 1990s. Although the United States has long supported and participated in a variety of international organizations and programs working on a variety of these problems, it has only recently begun to allocate a significant amount of its foreign aid explicitly for this purpose.

Table 4.2 Projected world population (thousands)

Region	1950	1998	2050
World	2,521	5,901	8,909
Africa	221	749	1,766
Asia	1,402	3,585	5,268
Latin America	167	504	809
Europe	547	729	628
North America	172	305	392
Oceania	13	30	46

Source: United Nations, Population Division, World Population Prospects: The 1998 Revision (New York: United Nations, 1998) and http://www.unfpa.org/.

Continuing increases in population, rising global prosperity, and intensifying urbanization will put further pressures on world resources in the years ahead. Addressing the transnational problems heightened by these pressures is likely to become a major purpose of US aid in the future.[5] Let us examine briefly the probable trends in population growth, prosperity and poverty, and urbanization in the new century.

The Trends: Population

On 12 October 1999, the "day of 6 billion" was observed—based on an estimate of the world population at that time. This was double the level of world population just 40 years ago. Each year, roughly 60 million are added to total world population, which is expected to rise to nearly 9 billion by 2050 (see table 4.2). Because of the spreading demographic transition, the increasing use of family planning services, and the impact of HIV/AIDS, the rate of population growth is slowing in most of the world—even in Sub-Saharan Africa, where population growth rates have long been among the highest worldwide. But the momentum of past population growth will continue to produce significant increases in world population well into the new century. These increases will be concentrated in some of the world's poorest countries and most fragile environments.

---

5. The increasing importance of transnational issues—or "international public goods"—as a world concern and as a purpose of foreign aid is examined in two excellent books: Inge Kaul, Isabelle Grunberg, and Marc Stern, eds., Global Public Goods: International Cooperation in the 21st Century, New York: Oxford University Press, 1999; and Ravi Kanbur and Todd Sandler with Kevin Morrison, The Future of Development Assistance: Common Pools and International Public Goods, Policy Essay 25, Washington: Overseas Development Council, 1999. Both these works emphasize the growing importance of transnational issues in the allocation and use of foreign aid.

In short, there has been considerable progress in reducing the rate of increase of world population as a result of the impact of rising incomes, expanding education (especially for women), and the spread of family planning services. But population is set to rise significantly into the middle of the new century—and, with it, the resulting pressures on world resources and the continuing challenges, especially in poor countries, for rapid economic progress.

Prosperity and Poverty

Looking back over the past half-century of global growth and development, it is hard not to marvel at the extraordinary progress that has been achieved in most parts of the world. Western Europe and Japan recovered from World War II to become among the most prosperous of countries. The foundations for development—physical infrastructure, education, and health services—have greatly expanded throughout the world. For example, primary school enrollment in most developing countries today (save those in Sub-Saharan Africa) averages nearly 100 percent, up in many countries from 60-80 percent only a quarter-century ago. Even in Sub-Saharan Africa, two-thirds of the eligible children are in primary school today, whereas only one in three was in primary school in the 1960s. The story with healthcare, roads, communications, and other necessities of economic progress is similar.

These advances have supported real progress in raising per capita incomes in much of the developing world. By the beginning of the 21st century, low-income countries (i.e., with less than $785 per capita annual income) were concentrated in Sub-Saharan Africa and South Asia. China, with the world's largest population, is no longer in the "low-income" category. Only three countries in Latin America (Haiti, Honduras, and Nicaragua), one in the Middle East (Yemen), four in Southeast Asia (Cambodia, Laos, Myanmar, and Vietnam) and seven in Central Asia and the Caucasus (Afghanistan, Armenia, Azerbaijan, Kyrgys Republic, Mongolia, Tajikistan, and Turkmenistan) remain low-income countries.[6] Available data show that growth rates in Armenia and the Kyrgys Republic have been healthy (at 5.6 percent in 1996-97 and 4.2 percent in 1997-98, respectively) and, if they continue, should lift these countries out of the low-income category in the coming decade or so. Azerbaijan's oil should, with good management, do the same for that country. Vietnam—benefiting from a large inflow of private investment in response to its policy reforms—could also soon rise from the ranks of low-income countries if it maintains and strengthens its economic reforms.

---

6. See World Bank, *World Development Report 1999/2000: Entering the 21st Century* (Washington).

Additionally, since the early 1990s, international private capital flows to developing countries have increased significantly, as we have seen. Roughly half of this flow was FDI, which is potentially important for long-term growth. And while nearly three-quarters of this FDI was concentrated in 10 of the larger or better-off developing countries,[7] many of the smaller, poorer developing countries experienced a significant increase in FDI. For example, El Salvador received only $2 million in FDI in 1990; by 1997, FDI had risen to $11 million. In 1990, Ghana benefited from $15 million in FDI; by 1997, FDI had increased to $130 million. In Sri Lanka, FDI rose from $195 million in 1990 to $430 million, despite a civil war.[8] The rising levels of FDI, spurred by economic policy reforms in poorer countries, including privatization of state-owned enterprises and improved transportation and communications services, meant that these countries no longer had to rely primarily on domestic savings and foreign aid to fund investment and long-term growth.

The Asian crisis created a serious but temporary interruption of favorable trends in the flow of private capital and growth in many developing countries. From an average 6.6 percent rate of growth in developing countries in 1996, average growth rates in developing countries reached only 2.1 percent in 1998. (This statistic does not include Eastern Europe and the newly independent states of the former Soviet Union, which experienced a -3 percent rate of growth that year.) World Bank forecasts for growth in developing countries for 1999 were 3 percent, and projections for the years 2000 and 2001 rose to 4.2 percent and 4.5 percent, respectively.[9] Thus, the long-term prospects for continuing economic progress in much of the developing world appear positive. But this positive growth scenario will add to the pressures on resources and on the global environment, as we shall see.

Even with the good news of economic progress in many parts of the world, it is still true that roughly 1.2 billion people, or just over one in five human beings, still live on $1 per day. Another 1.6 billion people live on $1 to $2 per day. Thus nearly half the world's population is still extremely poor. These poor are concentrated in three places: China, India, and Sub-Saharan Africa. The good news is that both China and India are far better positioned than at any time in the past to manage their own growth and emerge from poverty and have much greater access to the international capital that can help them do so. The bad news

---

7. Argentina, Brazil, Chile, China, India, Indonesia, Mexico, Malaysia, Poland, and Venezuela. See World Bank, *Global Development Finance 1998: Analysis and Summary Tables* (Washington, 1998), 20.

8. World Bank, *Global Economic Prospects and the Developing Countries* (Washington, 2000), table 1.1.

9. World Bank, *Global Development Finance 1999*, op.cit., 19.

is that the number of desperately poor in Africa is growing in absolute numbers and governments there typically lack the capacity and capital to address effectively the deepening deprivation of their people. Thus, the problem of poverty and underdevelopment that will continue to challenge the world community in the 21st century is in Sub-Saharan Africa. Further bad news is that it is now widely recognized that many of the problems of underdevelopment in that troubled region are self-inflicted—the result of poor policies, weak institutions, corruption, and abysmal leadership. Why such essentially political problems should be so widely shared in the region and what should be done about them is still little understood. But they do not appear to be problems that can be easily overcome with foreign aid. Indeed, there is some evidence that such aid, imprudently provided, can make institutional problems worse.[10] Thus, the development challenge in Africa is to figure out when and how best to help the Africans gain a better future for themselves, recognizing that the most central problems of development there are the least understood and may be least amenable to aid interventions.

Urbanization

Along with a rise in world population has come a rapid increase in urbanization, producing growth in the demand for housing, sanitation, social services, education, and employment in cities. Roughly half of the world's population now lives in urban areas. This proportion will rise to two-thirds, or over 5 billion people, by 2015.[11] The rapid rate of urbanization in developing countries is particularly striking. The proportion of populations in these countries living in cities is expected to double between 1990 and 2025, with the most rapid rate of urbanization continuing to occur in Africa. For example, by 2020, West Africa will be more than 60 percent urbanized, with 30 cities of 1 million or more inhabitants (compared with 6 in 1990). Between Benin City in Nigeria and Accra, Ghana, alone there will be 5 cities with a combined population of about 25 million.[12]

These three trends—the growth in population, prosperity, and urbanization—will produce rising demands for food (particularly the higher

10. See Sam Wangwe and Carol Lancaster, *Aid Dependence in Africa*, Washington: Overseas Development Council, forthcoming.

11. See Secretary General, *Critical Trends: Global Change and Sustainable Development*, New York: Department for Policy Coordination and Sustainable Development, United Nations, 1997, for these and other data on future trends. This report offers a very good summary of existing forecasts. It can also be found at http://www.un.org/dpcsd/dsd/trends.

12. Club du Sahel, *Preparing for the Future: A Vision of West Africa in the Year 2020*, Paris: DAC, Club du Sahel, 1995, x.

protein foods associated with rising incomes[13]), water, and energy, and will increase pressures on the environment and national health systems and on the global commons (e.g., the oceans or Antarctica—i.e., areas not under the jurisdiction of a government). How much of a problem for the United States and the world will issues of scarcity and transnational environmental and health problems be in the new century? And how well positioned is the world today to deal with those problems, either through market mechanisms or through international organizations and regimes?

Scarcity Issues

An important set of transnational issues involve scarcity: Will there be an adequate quantity of essential commodities to meet global demand in the new century, given the increase in population, incomes, and urbanization? The major scarcity issue in the probable world of the first part of the 21st century is water. Food, particularly fisheries, could become a scarcity issue if agricultural research and fisheries management prove inadequate. Energy will not likely become a scarcity issue in the foreseeable future, although energy use will continue to contribute to global warming.

Water. "The defining issue of the 21st century may well be the control of water resources. In the next 30 years, it is likely that water shortages will increase dramatically. While water supplies are dwindling because of groundwater depletion, waste, and pollution, demand is rising fast."[14] Thus began the foreword to a recent study on world water by one of the more prudent and respected food policy research institutes. If there is one commodity where the probability of future demand appears likely to outrun supplies, at least in a considerable part of the world, and where international arrangements for dealing scarcity are least advanced, it is water.

The demand for water stems from three sources—agriculture (which accounts for 70 percent of water usage), industry, and human consumption. Thus the demand for water will grow with increasing population, rising food production, and growing industrial activities in coming decades.

---

13. The impact of population growth and rising incomes on the demand for food is geometric rather than arithmetic because people tend to demand higher protein foods— i.e., meat rather than grains or roots and tubers—as their incomes increase. However, it takes on the average 2 pounds of grain to produce 1 pound of chicken meat and 4 or more pounds of grain to produce 1 pound of beef.

14. Per Pinstrup-Anderson, Foreword to Mark Rosegrant, *Water Resources in the Twenty-First Century: Challenges and Implications for Action*, Washington: International Food Policy Research Institute, 1997, v.

There is, of course, an abundance of water in the world. But 97 percent of it is in the oceans, and therefore too salty for human consumption or agricultural use without expensive desalinization processes. Only 1 percent of the remaining 3 percent of world fresh water supplies is available for use, the remainder being locked up in glaciers and icebergs or in inaccessible underground sources. The remaining 1 percent, from lakes, rivers, aquifers, and rainfall, is adequate to meet human demand, but it is not evenly distributed. Africa, parts of Asia, and Europe have considerably less water available per capita than North and South America.

Most water experts agree that "the world faces severe and growing challenges to maintaining water quality and meeting the rapidly growing demand for water resources"[15] and that in coming decades there are likely to be increasingly severe shortages of water in the Middle East, Africa, and parts of China and India. Projections of water supply and demand in the year 2025 show that 46 to 52 countries with a total population of 3 billion people will be water stressed. That stress is likely to have two consequences. First, less water will be available for irrigation, reducing food production in water-stressed countries. Second, less water will be available per person for domestic purposes, potentially contributing to health and sanitation problems. These consequences for food production and health make water scarcity a transnational issue.

A further transnational implication of water scarcity is the possible contribution of severe water shortages to international conflicts among riparian states, for example, countries sharing the Jordan, Mekong, Nile, and Tigris rivers. Differences over water diversion and use have already contributed to tensions between Syria and Turkey, Israel and Jordan, India and Pakistan, and Cambodia and its neighbors. Plans by the government of Sudan to control the flow of water in the southern part of the country contributed to the outbreak of civil war there. Because water is so essential to life and because it has no easy or cheap substitutes, water scarcity can become a life and death issue, and so is fraught with political danger.

What are the solutions to current and future water scarcities? One potential solution is increasing the supply of usable water. Discovery of underground sources, desalination of seawater, and transport of icebergs to water-scarce areas have all been raised as possibilities—each with its own problems, usually involving uncertainty or high cost. Putting user charges on water with subsidies for the poor is another potential element in an approach to ensuring adequate water supplies in the future.

---

15. Mark Rosegrant, Ibid., 1. See also David Seckler, Upali Amarasinghe, and Randolph Barker, *World Water Demand and Supply, 1990 to 2025,* Colombo: International Water Management Institute, 1998; Tom Gardner-Outlaw and Robert Engleman, *Sustaining Water, Easing Scarcity,* Washington: Population Action International, 1997; and Peter Gleick, ed., *Water in Crisis: A Guide to the World's Fresh Water Resources,* New York: Oxford University Press, 1993.

These and other elements in a water strategy are pricey. One estimate has the cost of ensuring adequate water worldwide at about $100 billion per year during the coming decade or so.[16]

The most promising approach involves more efficient use of available water supplies. Efforts to reduce evaporation of freshwater resources (e.g., from rivers and lakes) and more efficient use and reuse of water are two important approaches. The problem of water efficiency is in part a technical problem and in part a policy problem—for example, the pricing of water at highly subsidized rates in many countries. But there is also much we still do not know about the supply and use of water worldwide. Indeed, of all the transnational problems considered here, water is the most recent to gain the world's attention and the least well understood. Given its importance to human life, water is also possibly the most important transnational issue. An urgent task for the international community is evolving internationally acceptable norms governing the distribution and use of water among riparian states. This process is still in its early stages.

International arrangements to address water issues are both embryonic and rather confused. Water issues are not yet a global priority; there has been no recent international summit on water, as there has on other major transnational issues, although an international conference on water was hosted by the Government of the Netherlands in March 2000.[17] Indeed, debates continue about how to conceptualize and gather accurate data on water issues. And there is still only limited research on the supply, demand, and use of water, and as yet little international assistance to fund water research or conservation efforts. A number of multilateral organizations are addressing various aspects of international water issues, but no single organization is charged with examining all the major interrelated facets of water. In recent years, there has been an effort on the part of various countries and international organizations to create international water organizations. In fact, two have been created—both rather weak. The World Bank and the UNDP have created a Global Water Partnership, with a small headquarters in Stockholm. It has several regional technical advisory groups to generate proposals for

---

16. See Ismael Serageldin, Draft World Water Commission Report (10 February 2000, 21), vision report for the Second World Water Forum, March 2000, http://www. worldwaterforum. org/index2.html.

17. There have been two significant conferences on water in the past—the UN Water Conference of 1977 and the International Conference on Water and the Environment in 1992. But these conferences emphasized water quality rather than the problem of water scarcity. The Government of the Netherlands sponsored a World Water Day and an international conference in March 2000 to draw attention to world water issues and create a consensus for action to address those issues. As of this writing, the effects of this effort are unclear, but at a minimum, it did not produce the worldwide attention and agenda-setting impact of the larger, more prominent summits sponsored by the United Nations during the past decade.

water-oriented activities, to be funded with foreign aid. There is also the World Water Council, located in Marseilles, whose mission is to develop a long-term, strategic vision for world water resources. Funded by the governments of Canada, The Netherlands, Sweden, and other countries, it has convened several large meetings and consultations, including governments, private enterprises, NGOs, think tanks, international organizations, and others. The capacity of these organizations to address the multiple issues associated with water is as yet far from clear.

Research on water is also fragmented. The International Food Policy Research Institute studies governmental policies that affect the supply of and demand for water; the International Water Management Institute examines the technology of water use for irrigation; the World Bank and other aid agencies provide funding for water-related projects. In short, an effective international regime for water does not yet exist.

Water will take on an increasing priority as a transnational issue in the 21st century and will create rising claims against US foreign aid.

Food. Will there be enough food to feed the world's population in the coming century? The demand for food will rise with increasing population and economic growth. Will the supply of food rise to meet this demand? These are questions asked by those who worry about future scarcities in an increasingly crowded and prosperous world.

The answer at this point appears to be yes, at least for the first quarter of the century.[18] With a modest increase in cultivated land and irrigation (and improved management of existing irrigation facilities), advances in farming technologies and improved plants, and continuing efforts to eliminate diseases and pests that can wipe out crops and animals, food production can rise to meet the increase in the demand for food, projected at just over 40 percent for cereals by 2020.[19]

Much of the increased future demand for food will come from developing countries, whereas a significant portion of the projected increase in world food supply will undoubtedly come from farmers in industrial countries, such as the United States. Increases in food supply will likely

---

18. See, e.g., Per Pinstrup-Anderson, Rajul Pandya-lorch, and Mark Rosegrant, *The World Food Prospects: Critical Issues for the Early Twenty-First Century,* Washington: International Food Policy Research Institute, 1999 and United Nations, *Critical Trends: Global Change and Sustainable Development,* op. cit., chapter 4. The World Food Summit hosted by the Food and Agriculture Organization in Rome in 1996 also agreed that the world was capable of producing enough food for all (though it recognized that large numbers of people lacked the resources to obtain an adequate diet). However, not every one agrees that global food scarcities can be avoided in the coming decades. Lester Brown is not as optimistic about the ability of farmers to continue to expand their yields of grain in the face of rising demands deriving from increases in population. See, e.g., Struggling to Raise Cropland Productivity in *State of the World 1998,* eds. Lester Brown, Christopher Flavin, and Hilary French, Washington: Worldwatch Institute, 1998.

19. Pinstrup-Anderson, et al., op. cit., 10.

result from technological advances, arising in large measure from privately funded research. However, there is still considerable scope and an economic need for expanded food production in poor countries. If that expansion is to occur, much of it will have to come from agricultural research tailored to the particular conditions in those countries. Private firms have limited incentives to undertake such research since the market for the results of that research may be poor and unremunerative. Thus agricultural research to benefit poor countries and poor farmers will have to rely primarily on public funding, including aid from industrial countries, as it has been done in the past.

The problem of adequate food supplies in the coming century will for the major crops not be one of too little production, but rather one of distribution. Although the world will be able to produce enough food for its growing population, not all segments of that population will have enough income to purchase nutritionally adequate quantities of food. Projections suggest that rapid increases in population and slow increases in food production in much of Sub-Saharan Africa in particular will lead to requirements for large amounts of food imports. And if food production expands only slowly (as it has done during the past several decades) and economic growth remains relatively low in this region, there may be a rising need for food aid in the future to meet the minimum nutritional needs of Africans.

What sorts of international arrangements are needed to ensure that world food production and distribution in the new century are adequate? The international regime addressing food issues includes numerous international and bilateral organizations. Principal among the international agencies are the Food and Agriculture Organization (FAO) and the Consultative Group on International Agricultural Research (CGIAR). The FAO monitors food production and consumption worldwide and can signal impending crises or problems. It has established a Codex Alimentarius to govern the quality of food sold and traded, to which 123 countries have agreed. And it provides technical assistance on food issues to governments of developing countries. The World Bank, the International Fund for Agricultural Development, bilateral aid donors, and others provide funding to help developing countries strengthen their agricultural sectors. Rules and norms governing international trade in agricultural commodities have been negotiated under the auspices of the World Trade Organization (WTO), leading to decreases in protection and subsidization of agricultural production in recent years. The WTO monitors compliance with those rules.

Research on agriculture—on crops, animals, farming systems, policies, and management issues—is conducted by three sets of organizations— private agribusiness enterprises, national research facilities (often universities or publicly funded research institutes), and the 16-member institutes of CGIAR.

The need in the past for publicly funded agricultural research was based on the likelihood that private enterprises would not put money into research on crops or farming techniques that would not bring them a significant payoff. That meant that basic research (which was risky and often very expensive) or research on crops consumed in poorer parts of the world were not on the private research agenda. Research on genetically engineered crops of interest to rich countries has gained on the research programs of private enterprises. But basic research on the crops, the farming techniques, and the peculiar problems of agriculture in the poorer parts of the world—especially the tropics—remains of relatively little interest to private agribusiness. There will continue to be a need for publicly funded research in these areas if the poorer regions of the world are to meet at least a proportion of their food needs.

The main vehicle for this research will continue to be CGIAR. This network of separate and independent institutes, with an executive secretariat in the World Bank, has been relatively effective in the past in supporting expanded food production in the developing world (e.g., through the development and dissemination of high-yielding wheat and rice varieties that led to the Green Revolution), often in collaboration with national agricultural research systems in industrial and developing countries. CGIAR is currently funded with just over $300 million annually in foreign aid from the United States and other countries. Given the importance of technological advances in agriculture in developing countries for ensuring an adequate supply and distribution of food in the new century, the allocation of aid for this purpose will continue to have a high priority. Another priority will be for the public sector to seek out opportunities to collaborate with private agribusiness enterprises to develop and disseminate improved crops and farming practices that can help farmers in poor countries. This is not an easy task but a creative use of public funds, and perhaps tax incentives for private firms to research such crops could well produce valuable results.

In short, the international regime for addressing issues of food scarcity is in place. The task for the new century is to maintain it through ongoing funding of key activities, particularly research. This task will make a continuing demand on US aid in the new century.

Energy. With the increase in population, urbanization, and economic growth (in particular, industrialization) in the probable world of the new century, the demand for energy is expected to expand as well, doubling by the year 2030. Much of this increase is anticipated to come from rapidly developing countries, particularly in Asia.[20]

---

20. See US Department of Energy, *International Energy Outlook 1998*, Washington: US Government Printing Office. See also N. Nakkenovic, A. Gruebler and A. McDonald, *Global Energy Perspectives*, Cambridge: Cambridge University Press, 1998.

The supply of energy is projected to expand to meet rising demands, continuing as in the past to respond to market signals. Future energy supplies will be drawn primarily from fossil fuels, with reliance on natural gas increasing particularly rapidly. Renewable energy sources are also expected to increase—for example, biomass, wind, hydropower, and the fuel cell, once it becomes commercially viable.[21] Increasing supplies of energy are expected to keep energy prices from rising significantly in coming decades.[22]

The international regime of energy production, consumption, research, and development is primarily the market—private firms responding to market signals and opportunities. In the past, the market, in part propelled by rising energy prices of the 1970s and in part by the spreading privatization of energy production in the 1980s and 1990s, has worked to provide incentives to increase production (including the discovery and more efficient exploitation of oil reserves) and efficiency in the face of rising demand. The market has been supplemented by information on worldwide trends in energy production and use gathered by the International Energy Agency (part of the Organization for Economic Cooperation and Development) and the US Department of Energy. It has at times been reinforced by government regulations requiring greater efficiency in energy production and use.

Although issues involving energy supplies may present the United States with foreign policy challenges in the new century as a result of the relationship between oil and international politics, energy scarcity as such is not likely to be an issue that will make a significant demand on US aid resources. There is, however, a transnational energy problem facing the United States and the rest of the world in the new century: The impact on the environment of the burning of fossil fuels—both in the form of air pollution and the production of greenhouse gases. We shall address these issues below in the section on the environment.

Externalities

The other major category of transnational problems involves the adverse consequences (or negative externalities) of actions or conditions in one country for populations beyond their borders. The two most significant kinds of externalities involve the environment and health.

Environment. The most complex and challenging issues resulting from the increase in world population and prosperity involve the world environment. The impact of human activity in one country on land, water, and atmospheric resources can and often does have negative conse-

---

21. See, e.g., At Last, the Fuel Cell, *The Economist*, 25 October 1997, 89.

22. See US Department of Energy, op. cit.

quences not only for the inhabitants of that country but for populations in other, often distant lands. Serious international environmental problems have begun to become apparent in the past several decades. Among the most prominent are the reduction in the ozone layer and the increase in greenhouse gases, contributing to global warming, including loss of forests and biodiversity, pollution of water and air, depletion of world fisheries, and degradation of soil, contributing to desertification. Most of these problems are anticipated to worsen in coming decades, as forest cover continues to be reduced, plant and animal species become extinct, water and air pollution problems increase, and soil continues to degrade. And with the historically unprecedented numbers of people and level of prosperity in the world, additional environmental challenges, as yet unforeseen, could arise in the future, as they do almost on a weekly basis at present.

Addressing international environmental issues is particularly challenging because of the nature of those issues. They typically involve human activities, the social costs of which are often not captured in private costs or market prices. Indeed, social costs can be long run (even transgenerational), are potentially significant (especially where the negative impact of human activity proves irreversible), and often are not fully predictable. Finally, dealing with environmental problems frequently involves persuading or compelling individuals, firms, or governments to change their behavior in ways that carry immediate costs for them, often without offsetting benefits. Such changes can understandably provoke political resistance.

Addressing these challenges typically requires actions by governments, supported by the expenditure of public resources—for research to establish the nature and extent of the particular environmental problem and the technologies (especially low-cost ones) to address the problem; for technical assistance to help individuals, firms, and governments to adopt those technologies; and for side payments to provide incentives for behavioral change.

To what extent has the international community already put in place an international regime to deal with transnational environmental problems? The UN Environment Program (UNEP), set up after the world environmental conference in Stockholm in 1972 as the key international organization addressing environmental issues, has focused largely on gathering data. Perhaps because UNEP had come to be regarded by many governments as weak, in the wake of the UN Conference on the Environment and Development in Rio de Janeiro in 1992, another international body to convene and coordinate transnational environmental issues was created—the UN Commission on Sustainable Development. This body, made up of a number of UN member states, meets periodically to discuss environmental issues but does little else.

In fact, a number of separate international environmental regimes, at various stages of development, have begun to evolve.[23] There are, for example, more than 150 international treaties and protocols on different environmental issues. (The rules and norms included in many of these treaties are, however, often limited, and monitoring and enforcement are often nonexistent.) In a number of cases, regimes have evolved beyond treaties. Among the most successful is the effort to deal with the depletion of the ozone layer: 155 countries have agreed to the Montreal Protocol on Ozone Depletion, which regulates the use of chlorofluorocarbons and other chemicals that have been shown to lead to the depletion of the ozone layer. An international secretariat has been established to monitor problems of the ozone layer and compliance with the Montreal Protocol by signatories. A multilateral fund has been set up, financed by industrial countries and administered by the World Bank, to help poor countries develop alternatives to ozone-depleting chemicals. There is still some controversy as to the severity or even the existence of this problem, and efforts to address it are still in an early stage. Other major environmental issues that continue to challenge the international community include preserving biodiversity, protecting the world's forests (important for biodiversity protection and as carbon sinks to absorb greenhouse gases), and managing the world's water resources and fisheries.

Although some progress has been made in addressing these issues— for example, the creation of the Global Environment Facility (housed in the World Bank and described in appendix A) to help fund projects involving biodiversity preservation or reduction in greenhouse gases in poorer countries—there is still much to be done before effective regimes are in place. The area of international environmental issues is one where important transnational problems are still emerging (and are likely to continue to do so in coming decades); where the operation of the market is unlikely to address satisfactorily many of those issues (especially where information is limited, and costs are potentially high, evident only after a long period of time, and possibly irreversible); where some international regimes are effective and others weak or nonexistent; and where it is consistent both with US interests and values to take a leadership role in addressing these issues. That leadership is likely to require aid to fund research, provide incentives for governments to adopt needed reforms, and finance the equipment and training that will help protect the global environment.

Health. The major international concern in the area of health is the outbreak and international transmission of infectious disease. Thirty new diseases have emerged in the past two decades, including HIV/

---

23. For an excellent study of international environmental institutions, see Peter M. Haas, Robert O. Keohane, and Marc A. Levy, *Institutions for the Earth*, Cambridge, MA: MIT Press, 1993.

AIDS.[24] There have already been several outbreaks of deadly diseases in recent years that were long thought to be under control—cholera in Peru, the plague in India, diphtheria in Russia and the Ukraine, and drug-resistant tuberculosis in several regions (including within the United States). Several diseases that are always debilitating and sometimes deadly have also begun to regain ground after being controlled or eradicated from various regions—including leishmaniasis, dengue, and malaria. And most worrisome is the growing resistance of certain pathogens—such as malaria and tuberculosis—to prophylactic or curative drugs.

The outbreak of cholera in South America quickly spread well beyond the borders of Peru, showing the world how fast such diseases can be transmitted internationally through the rapid movement of people. The newest deadly disease is AIDS, with 23 million people infected in Africa alone and 11 million elsewhere in the world today. In some parts of Africa, life expectancy has dropped to below 50 years, with one-quarter of the adult population HIV-positive, making the disease nearly as rampant as the plague, which killed a third of the population of Europe in the 15th century. The disease continues to spread by more than 5 million cases per year and is increasing in Asia, Eastern Europe, and the former Soviet Union.

Environmental disturbances induced by climatic changes and the expansion of human habitation into scarcely inhabited areas cause previously unknown diseases to attack human populations. Large-scale migration of people can carry sicknesses far afield from their source. Finally, the pressures on public health services, particularly in the increasingly crowded urban areas of poor countries, can lead to the outbreak and spread of infection, both within poor countries and beyond their borders. These trends threaten to keep international health issues high on the world agenda—and the US agenda—in the new century.

Is there an effective international regime in the area of health? A critical element in such a regime are the health systems in individual countries. Do they provide adequate preventive healthcare, including inoculations against infectious diseases and education about diseases such as HIV/ AIDS for which there are no cures? Do they have the ability to monitor and respond to the outbreak of disease in their territories? Do they have the public infrastructure, especially in urban areas, that provides adequate sanitation to prevent the outbreak of disease?

We know the answers to these questions in poor countries: Their health systems are often limited and inadequate. The efficacy of health services is also questionable in countries in transition where those systems have collapsed. Where national health systems are inadequate, is there an

---

24. See World Resources Institute, *World Resources: A Guide to the Global Environment, 1998-99*, Washington: World Resources Institute, 1999, 3.

effective international regime to prevent, monitor, and respond to the outbreak of disease? The elements of such a regime exist in the area of monitoring and response. The WHO monitors disease outbreaks and coordinates responses. The Center for Disease Control in Atlanta also monitors the outbreaks of disease and provides expertise and research facilities (which WHO does not have) to determine the nature of disease threats and appropriate responses. But these and other organizations active in the area of controlling infectious diseases are described as "informal" and in need of strengthening: "The international community does not always have adequate resources to respond to localized disease outbreaks and control them before they can spread across borders."[25] Further, vaccines needed for responding to a disease outbreak can be scarce, that is, the "surge" capacity to provided needed drugs, vaccines, or antisera to meet a major outbreak of disease can be limited. This is an additional source of concern.[26]

With regard to prevention, a number of agencies, including USAID, UNICEF, and WHO, support inoculation programs in many developing countries, and coverage of children has been substantial. Funding on health education, especially in HIV/AIDS prevention, has also been provided by USAID, WHO, and other agencies, although much more could be done.

Where there appears to be a serious gap in the international health regime is in the assistance available to poor countries to establish effective health systems that would prevent or control the outbreak of disease in their own countries, and so keep disease from spreading beyond their borders. Inadequate clean water, sanitation, and public health facilities contributed to the outbreak of cholera in Peru in the early 1990s, as mentioned earlier. In the new century, the problem of minimally adequate public health facilities will be a particular challenge for the poorest developing countries experiencing the most rapid growth in population and urbanization. This challenge is not yet being met. It will continue to call on US aid resources in future years.

Globalization

The coincidence of rapidly expanding world trade, the dramatic increase in international capital flows, the internationalization of both corporate ownership and production (which has also fed the increase in interna-

25. Working Group on Emerging and Re-emerging Infectious Diseases, *Infectious Disease—A Global Health Threat*, Washington: Committee on International Science, Engineering and Technology, National Science and Technology Council, 1995.

26. Ibid., 30 ff.

Table 4.3 Foreign direct investment in the developing world
(net, billions of US dollars)

Region	1970	1980	1990	1997	1998
Latin America and the Caribbean	1.1	6.1	8.2	61.6	59.9
Sub-Saharan Africa	0.4	0.0	0.8	5.2	4.8
East Asia and Pacific	0.3	1.3	11.1	54.3	61.0
South Asia	0.1	0.2	0.5	4.7	4.4
Middle East and North Africa	0.3	−3.3	2.8	5.4	5.9

Source: World Bank, *Global Development Finance 1999, Analysis and Summary Tables* (Washington: World Bank, 1999), 190-203.

tional trade and capital movements),[27] and the instantaneous availability of vast amounts of information for those connected to the Internet—all are key elements in a world economy that is more economically integrated and interdependent than ever before. Factors facilitating the degree of global economic integration today are the openness of the world's economies, which has greatly increased during the past decade, and the enormous improvements in communications and transportation that have facilitated trade, capital flows, and transnational systems of production.

Expanding trade and international capital flows have contributed to increased growth in many developing countries. The foundations of growth —an adequate physical infrastructure and educated labor force, combined with growth-supporting policies and effective institutions (including, above all, the rule of law)—must necessarily be in place. With strong fundamentals, the inflow of foreign direct investment, foreign loans, and portfolio capital, together with increasing export opportunities deriving from a liberalized world trading system, provide the basis for rapid economic expansion. Indeed, developing countries throughout much of the world have enjoyed healthy growth for much of the past decade.

Tables 4.3 and 4.4 suggest that globalization has both benefits and costs for developing countries. Among the benefits is potential access to foreign direct investment and other forms of external capital at levels higher than anytime in recent history. The costs include the potential volatility of external capital flows—especially short-term flows that fled from several countries in East Asia in 1997, which led to slower growth there and, through "contagion," contributed to drops in both external

---

27. Perhaps the most novel aspect of globalization today is the location of various elements in corporate production processes in different countries, responding to wage and other advantages. Similarly, there has been an increase in international sourcing of intermediate inputs by corporate enterprises. See, e.g., Organization for Economic Cooperation and Development, *Globalization of Industry: Overview and Sector Reports*, Paris: Organization for Economic Cooperation and Development, 1996. This phenomenon has led to a rise in cross-border, intrafirm trade and financing.

Table 4.4 Economic growth in the developing world
(annual percentage change in GDP)

Region	1988-97	1996	1997	1998
Latin America and the Caribbean	2.6	3.4	5.1	2.0
Sub-Saharan Africa	2.3	4.2	3.4	2.1
East Asia and Pacific	8.8	8.8	6.5	1.8
South Asia	5.8	6.9	6.9	5.2
Middle East and North Africa	2.6	5.3	3.1	1.5

Source: World Bank, *Global Economic Prospects 1999* (Washington: World Bank, 1999), 152-71.

capital flows and growth in Latin America and elsewhere. Another major cost of globalization involves those left out or disadvantaged by the increasing integration of world markets. A final aspect of globalization we must consider briefly is its dark side—the enhanced ability it provides to criminals and terrorists to operate successfully.

Short-Term Volatility

With the recent financial crises in Mexico and Asia, the costs of volatility are now familiar. International commercial capital flows include a significant proportion of short-term capital, seeking opportunities for gain in exchange rate arbitrage or interest rate differentials in foreign countries; in returns from foreign stock or bond markets, derivatives and other international financial instruments; and in real estate speculation abroad. These international financial flows have proven highly mobile, moving rapidly and massively out of countries where investors perceive economic troubles. The end result is a worsening of those troubles. Where banking systems have proven weak, the regulatory environments poor, and governments unable or unwilling to manage capital inflows effectively, as in Indonesia, South Korea, and Thailand, economic downturns have provoked a flight of short-term capital, causing currency devaluations, credit crunches, debt servicing problems, and economic recession.[28] "Contagion"—fears on the part of investors that other emerging markets share similar problems—provoked outflows of capital from those markets (whether those fears are justified or not) and resulted in similar pressures on the exchange rates, equity, and other markets—and on the availability of credit in those countries.

Policy reforms, improved regulations, oversight, and greater transparency in the financial sectors of emerging markets is one part of the

---

28. See, e.g., Morris Goldstein, *The Asian Financial Crisis,* Washington: Institute for International Economics, 1998.

solution to the problems of short-term international capital volatility. Indeed, these types of reforms need to be largely in place before full financial liberalization takes place. Improved risk management by lenders is another element of reform. And more transparency and effective oversight on the part of the International Monetary Fund is a third element of needed reform. The need for these reforms appears to be increasingly recognized by the international community.[29]

Globalization's Losers

Globalization potentially has two kinds of losers. First are those groups within countries whose interests are hurt by globalization (e.g., the loss of their jobs) and those who believe globalization has a negative impact on the things they value (e.g., the environment or the preservation of culture). The second kind of losers are those countries not participating significantly in the globalizing world economy.

A number of analysts of globalization as well as political activists (evident at the abortive World Trade Organization meeting in Seattle in 1999) fear that increased trade liberalization will cause a loss of jobs to low-wage countries (where labor and environmental abuses may support lower costs of production) and that the greater mobility of capital vis-à-vis labor will be a disadvantage for labor in globalizing economies as firms and governments compete for export markets and foreign investment—and so place downward pressure worldwide on wages, benefits, and labor standards. Greater capital mobility may also force governments to compete for foreign investment with lower taxes, thus reducing their abilities to fund social insurance and other benefits for their own citizens. These threats constitute the now familiar "race to the bottom."

The adverse economic and social impacts of globalization predicted by its critics have not, according to available data, occurred. There is as yet little evidence of decreases in wages, worker benefits and standards, or tax efforts in the United States or elsewhere associated with efforts to attract foreign direct investment.[30] But politics is as much about

---

29. For an examination of the "international financial architecture" and recommendations for reforms that would help reduce the incidence and severity of international financial crises and enable the world community to manage them better, see Council on Foreign Relations, *Safeguarding Prosperity in an Global Financial System: The Future International Financial Architecture*, New York: Council on Foreign Relations, 1999.

30. Nic Van de Walle, *Economic Globalization and Political Stability in Developing Countries*, Washington: Rockefeller Brothers Fund, 1998. See also Dani Rodrik, *Making Openness Work*, Washington: Overseas Development Council, 1999. Rodrick agrees, citing evidence, that the trade and investment liberalization associated with developing countries' integration into the global economy has increased rather than decreased the demand for skilled labor in those countries. However, economic openness has also led to widening disparities in wealth and income in many countries.

perceptions as realities, and the perception—especially in the United States —of many labor unions, human rights and environmental groups, and others is that globalization is a threat both to their values and interests. These groups are active and vocal and have allied to create a growing opposition to policies—particularly, trade liberalization—identified with globalization. They may have also created a focus for a broader populist movement, at the core of which is a hostility to large institutions (the banks were the object of that hostility in the last century) and powerful, impersonal forces. As Hufbauer has observed, the "battle of Seattle" could mark a turning point rather than a rest stop on the road to globalization if the backlash to it continues to increase.[31] The United States will want to manage globalization's backlash—especially within the United States itself—by addressing the issues of human and labor rights, health issues, and the environmental degradation deriving from increasing trade and investment abroad, around which the antiglobalization coalition has formed.

Turning to the problem of whole countries losing out in a globalizing world economy, those lacking adequate infrastructure and human capital as well as the policy and institutional environments will be unable to attract international investors (or, even more important, encourage their own citizens to invest) or to compete in international markets. As a result, they will be unable to benefit from the economic growth associated with expanding trade and investment. This appears to be a particular problem for most countries in Sub-Saharan Africa, where there have been only small increases in international capital inflows or external trade during the past decade and where growth rates remain modest. The challenge of joining the globalization bandwagon for these countries is much the same as the challenge of development: They need to get their policies right and ensure that their institutional environment is supportive of private investment and equitable growth.

Globalization's Dark Side

The dark side of globalization is well known. The vast amount of information now available to terrorists and the ability of criminals, drug lords, and terrorists to act beyond their borders and coordinate with one another is documented.[32] The challenge to the United States and other governments now is to develop the technologies and capacity

---

31. See Gary Hufbauer, World Trade after Seattle: Implications for the US, International Economic Policy Briefs, Institute for International Economics, Washington, December 1999, http://www.iie.com/newsletr/new99.10htm.

32. See, e.g., Frank Cilluffo, ed., *Cybercrime . . . Cyberterrorism . . . Cyberwarfare*, Washington: Center for Strategic and International Studies, 1998; Frank Cilluffo and Linnea Raine, eds., *Global Organized Crime: The New Empire of Evil*, Washington: Center for Strategic and International Studies, 1994.

to act together to deal with the dark side of globalization. The United States is already putting nearly half a billion dollars into fighting drugs and terrorism and stemming the spread of weapons of mass destruction. This use of US concessional resources abroad—which we have not included in our definition of foreign aid—will surely expand in coming decades.

Policy Implications

What are the implications of globalization for US foreign aid? Surprisingly, perhaps, given the importance of the technological revolution and increasing integration of the world, there appear to be relatively few new claims on US foreign aid generated by the process of globalization. Short-term financial volatility will demand a US financial response where it is threatening to the international economy. But the combination of an effective International Monetary Fund and, where necessary, use of the Exchange Stabilization Fund managed by the Treasury (which provides the administration with the authority in cases of extraordinary need to provide large-scale, short-term financing for financial support operations abroad)[33] should be adequate to address future financial crises associated with globalization. Proposals for the establishment of a large-scale, aid-funded worldwide safety net to off-set the impact of financial volatility on the poor in affected countries are impractical and possibly unwise. The necessary funding would be hard to find, and they could create a moral hazard (i.e., inadvertently discourage responsible financial behavior on the part of governments and their creditors by promising to relieve them of the consequences of their failures) while drawing funding away from other urgent uses for foreign aid.

With regard to globalization's losers, the challenge for entire countries of being able to exploit the advantages of rising private investment and trade is much the same as the basic development challenge: The foundations of development must be in place—adequate physical infrastructure and a healthy and educated population—including a policy and institutional environment that is supportive of investment. These uses of foreign aid are not new.

With regard to groups within countries that are hurt by globalization, they present challenges to individual governments, but challenges that do not make a claim on US foreign aid. With regard to the apparently growing fear that globalization will lead to more environmental degradation or encourage rapacious and brutal treatment of labor, these are essentially

---

33. For more information on the Exchange Stabilization Fund, which the Treasury used to finance the Mexican rescue package in 1995 and fund US support for several countries affected by the Asian financial crisis, see C. Randall Henning, *The Exchange Stabilization Fund: Slush Money or War Chest?*, Washington: Institute for International Economics, 1999.

regulatory issues that will require international negotiation but not significant amounts of US foreign aid.

Purposes of Foreign Aid in the 21st Century

This chapter has identified two major purposes of US aid in the 21st century—peacemaking and addressing transnational issues. Humanitarian relief will remain an important purpose and, as argued in previous chapters, humane concerns will enjoy a place of growing prominence. What role should promoting development abroad play in the future of US foreign aid?

It will be remembered that foreign aid for promoting economic development in poor countries was initially justified on several grounds (in addition to those related to the Cold War): Developing countries were too poor to finance their own development, except at an unacceptably slow rate, and there were few international private sources of development financing. Further, with the basic foundations of development—infrastructure and education in particular—still lacking, developing countries would not be attractive for private investors, even if such investment were available.

In much of the developing world, these conditions no longer hold, as we have observed earlier. Domestic savings and investment rates have risen significantly in much of Asia and Latin America, and international commercial capital flows (albeit still relatively small in many developing countries) have surged, particularly during the past decade. Transportation and communications infrastructure has expanded enormously since the 1950s and 1960s, when aid for development first became a significant purpose of US foreign policy. Basic education is now available for most of the eligible age groups in much of Asia and Latin America. (The average proportion of the eligible age group in primary school was between 90 and 99 percent in Latin America and East Asia in 1995.[34]) And governments in many of these countries exhibit far greater capacity to manage their own economic progress effectively than ever in the past. In short, much of the original rationale for foreign aid for development in much of Asia and Latin America is now obsolete, thanks to the real economic progress there.

Some readers will object that the enormous poverty in Asia and Latin America still justifies US aid for development in these areas. There is still great poverty in these regions. However, US aid was never intended by itself to eradicate poverty (and never large enough to do so), but rather to help countries reach the point at which they could grow, manage their

---

34. World Bank, *World Development Report 1998-99*, New York: Oxford University Press, 1998, 200-01.

economies, and eradicate their own poverty. This is one of the messages of the much retold tale of the importance of teaching a man to fish rather than to give him fish every day. Many countries are now at that point. This does not mean that there is no longer any rationale for aid for non-concessional lending by the multilateral development banks to countries such as Brazil or India. This kind of lending (not foreign aid as defined here, but often thought of as foreign aid) can still supplement these governments' own efforts. But it is difficult to make the case that grant aid or highly concessional lending should still be provided to spur development in the more industrialized developing countries—even those with large pockets of poverty—because the governments of those countries have the capacity and the potential access to funding from domestic and international sources to address those problems themselves. They are—as is often said—rightly now "in the driver's seat" of their own economic progress.

There is, however, an important caveat to the argument that the purpose of using aid to promote economic development in poor countries will be far less important in the 21st century than in the 20th. As we have noted, there are still roughly 50 countries, primarily in Sub-Saharan Africa, along with a number in Latin America and Asia, where the basic foundations of growth and development are not yet adequate, where private investors have been reluctant to risk their capital, and where a significant amount of foreign aid (provided an appropriate policy environment is in place) is still justified on traditional developmental grounds.

Promoting Democracy

Promoting democracy, reflecting US values, is likely to remain a purpose of US foreign policy for the foreseeable future. But its role in US foreign policy and the particular activities it involves will change. During the past decade, US support for democracy abroad was highly visible and at times controversial, because it involved establishing the international legitimacy of democracy over alternative forms of government and because it included pressures on authoritarian governments to adopt liberalizing reforms. This stage of promoting democracy abroad is now largely over, for the ideal (if not always the reality) of democratic governance is now widely accepted internationally. Few national leaders are willing at present to justify nondemocratic governing structures, even where they in fact exist. And many countries have now implemented democratic reforms, including a free press, multiparty competition, and often a first and even second national election.

However, many countries have the facade of democratic institutions without the substance. Opposition political parties are weak, fragmented, often harassed, and ill prepared to challenge governments. Exposés of corruption in the press bring no action by government or by a cowed or disinterested public. Judicial systems are often strongly influenced by politicians or weak in their support of the rule of law. Political power remains concentrated in the hands of the ruling party and president. Civil society organizations are often limited, inexperienced, and reliant on outside funding to survive. As a result, promoting democracy now entails less supporting a transition to democratic institutions and more consolidating those institutions and helping them work effectively. Although these tasks are far less visible or productive of quick or dramatic results, neither do they require significant amounts of aid (because they primarily involve advice and training). Indeed, they may require considerably less aid than has been spent on promoting democracy in the past, for they will involve fewer of the big-ticket items of funding elections (which can cost tens of millions of dollars). However, they are far more complex, risky, and controversial, and must take place over the long term.

Much less is known about how to make illiberal democracies more liberal: The issues involve not only political or legal reform but often broad social change as well, and include levels of education, political culture, ethnicity, the distribution of income and wealth, and a host of other factors. These will be tasks of the future of democracy promotion and the use of US aid to pursue that purpose. In short, democracy promotion will remain a purpose of US foreign policy and US aid in the new century. It will pose difficult challenges to the United States to realize this purpose, but this purpose will not be a major one, at least in the resources it will require.

Promoting Economic and Political Transitions

We have not included this current purpose as one that will continue to exist into the new century, assuming that the northern tier of countries in Eastern and Central Europe will have largely completed their transitions to free markets and democracy—or at least will have reached the point where they no longer need foreign aid for those purposes—in the coming half-decade. Some, such as Estonia, already have "graduated" from US foreign aid. Others, such as the poorer countries in Central Asia, may complete their transitions but could still require foreign aid for traditional development purposes. Presumably, US aid for that purpose will come from bilateral or (more likely) multilateral assistance programs. For those potentially well-off countries, like Russia or the Ukraine, which have failed to achieve vigorous and effective programs of economic and political transition, foreign aid may again prove to be relevant once they are on the road to political and economic reforms. And there are still a few countries yet to begin a transition—for example, Cuba. But transition aid, even for them, would presumably be needed only for a limited period, until investment rises and their economies begin to expand.

Summing Up

What the findings in this chapter suggest about the future of US foreign aid is, first, there will be four major purposes of that aid: Supporting a policy of peacemaking; addressing transnational issues; providing humanitarian relief; and advancing humane concerns abroad. These are different from the priorities of the past, although US aid appears to be evolving in their direction (albeit more by happenstance than design). Other, less prominent purposes in the new century include promoting democracy, supporting development, and helping with economic and political transitions.

In chapter 3, we identified a purpose of US foreign aid that has taken on increasing importance in the past decade or so: Humane concerns—that is, providing foreign aid directly to beneficiaries in disadvantaged communities and vulnerable groups to help improve the quality of their lives. Such aid interventions may involve, for example, inoculating children, funding micro-enterprise loans to poor women, providing those wounded in war or from mines with prosthetics, and helping street children and AIDS orphans. It seems highly likely that the factors that have given increasing prominence to humane concerns in the recent past are likely to intensify in the future and further raise their importance.

There are three such factors. First is the associational revolution that has occurred during the past decade, both in the United States and in the rest of the world.[35] Political liberalization in many countries has encouraged the formation of NGOs to achieve a variety of interest-based and value-oriented goals and to press governments to act to support those goals as well. Protecting the environment is one such goal. Improving the status and influence of women is another. There are many others. Such groups have long been a characteristic of the US political landscape. But even in the United States, their numbers and activism have grown.[36]

A second factor enabling and encouraging political activism is the revolution in communications technology. The Internet provides individuals and groups with access to a vast amount of information to help inform their causes and the means by which they can network with other groups at home or abroad with similar concerns. A number of transnational movements among NGOs have taken shape and have exerted considerable influence—the international support for a treaty limiting the use of landmines in war is but one prominent example. And while early concerns that cross-national NGO activism meant the decline in the relative power

---

35. The term is Lester Salamon's. See his article, The Rise of the Nonprofit Sector, *Foreign Affairs* 73, no. 4 (July/August), 1994, 109-123.

36. Ibid., 111.

of states seem premature, these groups are undoubtedly a more potent factor in US and world politics today because of the Internet.[37]

Another change in the world has likely fueled policy activism in the United States and elsewhere: The end of the Cold War eliminated a major security threat to the United States and the world. That change, in turn, reduced the importance of security on the US foreign policy agenda and opened up space for other concerns. It also removed the pressures to compromise other international concerns in the face of a potential threat to the survival of the United States. Thus, the opportunity to put value-based issues on the US policy agenda (and by implication, to put US aid behind such issues, if appropriate), together with the increased numbers and activism of value-oriented NGOs evident in recent years, promise to continue to make humane concerns an important purpose in US foreign aid in the future.

This chapter has argued that the principal purposes of US foreign aid in the new century will be four—peacemaking; addressing transnational issues, among which international health and water scarcity are likely to claim urgent attention; providing humanitarian relief; and promoting humane concerns. Supporting economic development and promoting democracy will continue as purposes of US aid but with less priority than in the past. Supporting economic and political transitions will diminish as those transitions are complete.

These purposes do not come without their own particular challenges, substantive and political. With regard to peacemaking, if future administrations are to take the lead in this area and back up that leadership with foreign aid, they will need to build a measure of domestic political consensus around a policy of peacemaking. There is no such consensus at present. To gain that consensus, the administration will have to articulate a policy of when and where the United States will take the lead in peacemaking and when and where it will not.

With regard to using aid to address transnational issues, there is the problem of dealing with one set of problems—for example, addressing international health threats through strengthening public health systems in poor countries—without addressing all the problems in foreign societies that contribute to the particular transnational problem. Put simply, how can the United States hope to deal with international public health threats emanating from poor countries without dealing with their development challenge as a whole? This is a legitimate concern. The answer must be that the problems of international health—or protecting the environment or dealing with international crime—cannot wait until economic and social development is substantially achieved. They need to be addressed now. And willingness by external funders to address these

---

37. See Margaret Keck and Kathryn Sikkink, *Activists Beyond Borders*, Ithaca, NY: Cornell University Press, 1998, for a detailed examination of this important phenomenon.

issues could encourage developing-country governments to put a priority on them as well.

The challenges ahead for humanitarian relief are two. The first is to ensure to the extent possible that such relief is provided in a way that does not prolong the disaster it is trying to relieve. Experience shows that such relief can feed and encourage criminals as well as their victims—as in the case of the massive relief effort for Rwandan refugees in the Democratic Republic of the Congo in the wake of the genocide in Rwanda. Relief aid, if not prudently delivered, can also become the object of competition and conflict, as it was for the warlords of Somalia. The second challenge is to work out the relationship of humanitarian aid to broaden US foreign policy goals. This issue surfaced in 1999 when the idea was floated by officials in the Department of State that the United States should provide food aid to the rebel armies in southern Sudan. Although this idea was sharply criticized by relief groups, it was thought advantageous for political reasons by some in the administration. With the continuing conflicts in the world and US involvement in peacemaking, this issue is likely to become more pressing in the future.

A challenge to the use of US aid to address humane concerns is how such concerns are to be addressed in a sustainable fashion, without simply helping a few disadvantaged people for a short period of time. Although the intent of aid for this purpose is not, as we observed above, to make a strategic intervention in a country to support long-term economic and social development, these more modest efforts need to be planned and executed insofar as possible to provide for the sustainability of their impact. For example, one needs not only to deliver prosthetics to war-maimed individuals but also to seek to strengthen a community's ability to manufacture its own prosthetic devices. One needs to plan children's inoculations in a way that governments or community groups will eventually be able to take over the responsibility for delivering those inoculations. The relationship between addressing humane concerns immediately and directly versus laying the groundwork for their being addressed effectively by communities and groups abroad is a challenge for this purpose.

5

Organizing for a New Century

We can now draw together the themes and findings in the previous chapters to answer the question on how the United States should use its concessional resources to promote its interests and values in the new century. The major purposes will be four—peacemaking, addressing transnational issues, responding to humanitarian crises, and addressing humane concerns. The other purposes of the 20th century—promoting development, supporting economic and political transitions, and furthering democracy—will not disappear. But they will play a less prominent role in US foreign aid.

These purposes are consistent with the politics of aid as they have evolved during the past decade and contain the elements of a new policy paradigm. Two of the purposes—peacemaking and addressing transnational issues—are linked primarily to US interests, and two—humanitarian relief and addressing humane concerns—are linked to US values. At present, there is no consensus in Congress or among the public on the extent of a US policy of peacemaking abroad. However, a new administration willing to articulate such a policy and persuade Congress and the American people of its importance could combine that with the three other purposes for a potentially compelling new policy paradigm for foreign aid on which to build a strong future constituency.

The remainder of this chapter will focus less on the purposes of US aid in the future and more on the organization and management of that aid.

The Organization of US Aid in the New Century

How are we to organize our foreign aid programs to address their various purposes most effectively? A basic concept in public administration is that form should follow function. Those programs with similar purposes should be located in the same organization. When programs with very different purposes are housed together, it is often the case that the larger, more compelling purposes and programs overwhelm the less compelling ones. This has long been the reason that a number of governments separate development agencies from ministries of foreign affairs. Development agencies have as their mission the promotion of long-term economic and social change in foreign countries, which requires them to plan their activities years in advance, and work not just with governments but with a variety of private organizations and groups in the developing country. Ministries of foreign affairs tend to have much shorter time horizons as they attempt to manage bilateral relations with other countries—and, in particular, crises that erupt in those relations. Further, ministries of foreign affairs are almost always much more powerful than aid agencies, which seldom have a cabinet-level rank.[1]

A second problem in organizing US foreign aid is coordination. I refer here not to the age-old problem of coordination among multiple aid agencies operating in the field, which continues to be a major challenge. The coordination problem addressed here is coordination within the US government of the various agencies operating in the same countries abroad or addressing similar transnational issues.

The US government provides foreign aid for different purposes, but those often bear some policy relationship to one another and sometimes overlap in the types of activities funded. To ensure that the aid from different agencies at a minimum is consistent and, at best, is efficient and mutually reinforcing, coordination among aid agencies and programs, preferably within an overall planning framework, is important.[2] It will

---

1. The British and German governments are the major exceptions to this rule. Their main development agencies are cabinet-level agencies. The organization of British aid has been especially interesting and changeable over the past half-century. Depending on which political party was in power, its aid was either in the Foreign Office (under a Conservative government) or independent of the Office (under a Labor government). The multiple changes in the organizational location of British aid made little difference in the operation of that aid—but that was because when aid operations were housed in the Office, they were still quite distinct in personnel and management from other parts of the Office, and because British diplomats, who had a high regard for aid officials, tended to minimize their interference in the allocation and implementation of foreign aid. For more on these issues, see Carol Lancaster, *Aid to Africa*, Chicago: University of Chicago Press, 1999.

2. I wish to make a distinction here between coordination and integration. Senior aid officials often talk about integrating their various programs to ensure maximum impact. This is a worthy but unrealistic objective. Efforts at integrating multiple aid-funded activities in the past have often resulted in time-consuming red tape and poorly focused and managed activities that have resulted in failure. It is hard enough for separate bureaucratic entities to coordinate their programs, even in the most competent of governments. Real programmatic integration is often beyond the capacity of those governments,

be even more important in the future with the increasing involvement of multiple US government agencies in providing assistance abroad. We shall return to this point momentarily.

The first issue in the organization of US aid for a new century involves the division of labor between bilateral and multilateral aid agencies. In chapter 2, we mentioned the notional division of labor between these two types of agencies: Bilateral aid for those purposes closely associated with US interests and values that may be quite distinct from those of other countries; and aid for multilateral agencies when there is an issue of common concern among member states that requires their support to resolve. Within multilateral agencies, there is a logical division of labor as well: Multilateral development banks would focus on traditional development work, and international organizations would address transnational issues. The current organization and operation of bilateral and multilateral aid agencies, with their many overlapping programs and mission creep, have blurred many of these distinctions.

However, these basic distinctions still provide a guide for the organization of US aid in the new century. Bilateral aid should still be used for those purposes closely associated with US national interests and values and to back up US leadership in the world. These purposes include peacemaking, humanitarian relief, humane concerns, and—where international organizations do not exist or cannot effectively address them—transnational issues. Aid for development is best located primarily in the multilateral development banks that have the overall resources and the expertise to promote economic and social change in poor countries. (And the United States should encourage these organizations to make that purpose their main one.) Aid (i.e., technical assistance) for addressing transnational issues should be located primarily in international organizations with the capacity to call the world's attention to their issues, monitor the evolution of those issues, and provide help and encouragement to countries to address them. Unfortunately, for a number of transnational issues, international organizations either do not yet exist (as in the case of water) or are lacking in effectiveness. The problem with a number of UN organizations often starts at the top. Poor leadership, frequently chosen by one or a group of member states as their right, means that an entire organization is often unable to function effectively. Up to several years ago, weak leadership in the WHO nearly wrecked the good work WHO could do. And once an organization has been weakened by poor leadership, it can be very difficult and time consuming to renew its capacity and effectiveness. As part of its overall approach to transforming US aid and reforming the United Nations, the United States should support a process of leadership selection that is much more carefully vetted by

---

let alone the weak governments typical of the developing world. Many of the best intentions of aid planners in the past have foundered on the rocks of integration.

experts. International organizations are likely to take on much more importance in the future in addressing trans-national issues. They must have the capacity to do their job.

How should the United States organize its bilateral aid for the new century? Bilateral aid for purposes central to US foreign policy should be located in the agency responsible for those policies. Peacemaking and addressing transnational issues are prominent elements in US diplomacy. Promoting democracy abroad and supporting economic and political transitions are also US foreign policy goals, though they are foreseen to have less prominence in the future. Aid for these purposes should be located in the Department of State. Within the State Department's Global Affairs Bureau, there is already considerable expertise on democracy and transnational issues. Aid for peacemaking could be located in the Bureau of Political Military Affairs or in a central fund within the Office of Plans, Programs and Budgets. In practical terms, funding in USAID for transnational issues (population, health, environment and energy, democracy, and agricultural research funding) would be shifted to the Department of State. To ensure that the use of these funds and the policies governing them are well informed from a scientific point of view, the department should form a series of scientific advisory committees that would periodically review overall policies in these areas as well as the allocation and use of these funds.

Aid for humanitarian relief and aid for humane concerns should be located in a separate agency. This would ensure that decisions on these essentially value-based programs were made in consultation with foreign affairs agencies but independent of day-to-day foreign policy concerns. In practical terms, this agency would be made up of what is now the OFDA and the Office of Transition Initiatives in USAID, and the Refugee and Migration programs now located in the Department of State. Additionally, this agency would include funding in USAID (for microenterprises, child survival, helping street children, HIV/AIDS orphans, war victims, etc.) for the types of humane concerns described in chapter 2. And it would absorb the African Development Foundation and the InterAmerican Foundation, which do much the same type of work in their respective regions. The Peace Corps could also be folded into this new agency. But given its rather different modus operandi of recruiting and managing US volunteers in the field and the exceptionally strong constituency of ex-volunteers who would surely oppose strongly its being absorbed by another agency, it is probably best left independent.

How would the Department of State and the new aid agency manage their programs? It is often said by USAID officials (and many officials in the Department of State as well) that the State Department lacks the capacity to manage well a spending program involving planning, design, procurement, implementation and evaluation. While it does manage a sizable Refugee Program and other, smaller programs at present, absorbing a substantial portion of the programming responsibilities currently under USAID's control would certainly require the department to strengthen significantly its capacity for program management.

How would the new aid agency operate? The part dealing with humanitarian crises and their aftermath would continue as it has in the past, reacting rapidly and flexibly to organize and deliver relief to the victims of disaster and help them recover. The part of the new agency dealing with humane concerns would operate quite differently from USAID but similarly to the two government foundations that it absorbed. It would identify the broad areas in which it would work, including those (such as micro-enterprise funding and child survival) mentioned above, and accept proposals from US and foreign NGOs, enterprises, and governments to fund activities in these areas. It would seek funding partners from the private sector, including private voluntary organizations, community groups, foundations, and private enterprises working abroad. It could leverage private monies for its programmatic priorities and also help connect US groups with organizations in other countries, thus engaging the broader American public directly in worthy activities beyond our borders. The new agency would not have the elaborate strategic programming process now used by USAID and other development agencies, which in any case would be inappropriate for its purposes and the probable size of its resources. Rather, it would emphasize flexibility and creativity in its efforts to address humane concerns abroad. It would not require a sizable field presence to manage its activities, although it would demand high standards of program quality and accountability.

These changes would bring the organization and management of US aid in the new century into line with the purposes of that aid. However, they would not eliminate the problem of coordination among US government agencies providing aid abroad. The engagement of domestic government agencies in activities in foreign countries is likely to be a permanent and growing feature of US aid in the new century. It is a beneficial one as well, for it responds to the realities of a globalizing world. But it carries with it two challenges of coordination: One involving aid interventions in particular countries, especially where US relationships are sensitive; and the other involving strategies for addressing particular global issues.

Interagency coordination often seems more like warfare than cooperation. That is because there are usually few incentives for agencies to truly collaborate. In fact, the incentives—particularly for aid agencies— often run in the opposite direction—to resist collaboration that would impinge on their agency's autonomy and budget. There are, however, two potential sources of incentives that can encourage effective coordination—attention and pressure from the White House, and putting the authority for decision making for funding in interagency groups. Both of these approaches could be useful in creating an environment of coordination among US government agencies on transnational issues. On issues of aid coordination in countries of high priority, a group led by the NSC would be important to ensure that all US aid interventions are mutually supportive. This is to some extent the nature of interagency coordination for the bi-national commissions, led in this case by the vice president. This type of coordination cannot occur for all of the more than 150 countries to which the United States is accredited. But for the 25 or so high-priority countries, it will be unavoidable.

Coordination among agencies on strategies to address key transnational issues could be led by the Department of State or another appropriate cabinet-level agency. These interagency coordination efforts could be made effective if the Department of State and other participating agencies brought some resources to the table that they were empowered to allocate together. The resources themselves would create an incentive for coordination. There is a model for this approach in the old food aid committee chaired by the Department of Agriculture, with participation by the Department of State, USAID, OMB, and other agencies. The power to allocate food aid (and for any agency to veto a particular program) gave that committee real clout and its key members a serious reason not just to coordinate but to negotiate and work together.

Getting From Here to There

Assuming a new administration wanted to implement the proposals described above, how would it go about doing so? What it would *not* do is create an interagency working group, ask for ideas, try to get consensus, draft and clear legislation based on that consensus, and seek congressional support for the legislation. Past experience proves that such an approach takes forever and almost always ends up supporting the status quo.

What a new administration interested in transforming US foreign aid should do is create a small, expert working group, preferably reporting to the president (or even to the president-elect), to develop a detailed blueprint of the policy and organizational changes it plans to seek in US foreign aid. (Recommendations involving significant organizational and legislative changes would likely require a president to garner congressional support for those changes.) The blueprint should then be discussed with a limited number of senior career officials of the major agencies affected by the changes. Outside experts seldom have the day-to-day experience and detailed knowledge that career officials have of how policies and programs work; those outsiders must be willing to draw on inside knowledge and experience in an open-minded and judicious fashion if their organizational changes are to work and have legitimacy within the bureaucracy.

Consultations and negotiations with key members of Congress on the proposed changes are also essential. Those key members include the chairs and ranking members of the minority party of the Senate Foreign Relations Committee and the House International Affairs Committee and the chairs and ranking members of the foreign operations subcommittees of the appropriations committees of both the House and Senate. There may be other key members with an interest in foreign aid or who are part of the leadership of either house who should be part of a negotiation on a redirection and reorganization of US foreign aid. If a package of changes acceptable to these members and to the administration can be put together, much of the political task of bringing about a transformation of US aid will have been accomplished.

A further group that would need to be consulted on significant change in US foreign aid are the organizations that lobby for that aid and often implement it abroad—key country-focused groups and NGOs active in relief and development. Their political support is important, and many of them have detailed knowledge of how US aid actually works (and sometimes does not work) in the field. Their contribution could thus strengthen the proposed changes.

The process described here should ideally be implemented in the first 6 months of a new administration and before political appointments are made to the agencies most effected by the changes. If a process of significant organizational change drags on for many months, resistance to that change will grow and ultimately undermine its extent or usefulness. If 'tis to be done, 'tis to be done quickly.

The changes proposed in US foreign aid here are substantial. They would require considerable effort on the part of any administration to implement. But in transforming US foreign aid, they would bring it into the 21st century, clarifying its purposes and fortifying its relevance to US interests and values in a new world. The alternative is aid programs with unclear goals, overlapping mandates, declining relevance, and inappropriate programmatic and organizational arrangements—possibly eventually leading to a collapse in political support for them. This would be tragic, given the potential contribution of foreign aid to US interests and values, and the well-being of many abroad.

Appendices

Appendix A: A Brief Description of Organizations Funded by US Aid

Bilateral Aid Organizations

The United States funds four bilateral aid agencies: The US Agency for International Development (USAID), the Peace Corps, the InterAmerican Foundation, and the African Development Foundation. *USAID* is the largest of the four, managing aid programs of about $7 billion annually, including Development Assistance, food aid, Economic Support Fund (ESF) monies, and aid for the countries of Eastern Europe and the former Soviet Union. USAID has the lead on policies and country allocations of Development Assistance and a major role in decisions on food aid. The Department of State plays a major role in decisions on country allocations of ESF and funding for transitions in Eastern Europe and the former Soviet Union.

The *Peace Corps* works in a number of areas that correspond to the various purposes described in the previous chapter, including development, humane concerns, and humanitarian relief. It had a budget in fiscal year 2000 of $245 million, with volunteers working in 80 countries as teachers, community development specialists, and health, environmental, and agricultural experts. In 1996, it created a Crisis Corps to provide short-term assistance during humanitarian crises and disasters.

The *InterAmerican Foundation* and the *African Development Foundation*, both government organizations, work at the community level in Latin

America and Africa, supporting local NGOs and individuals in a variety of activities. Their budgets for fiscal year 2000 were $5 million and $14 million, respectively.

Most *other federal agencies* operate their own foreign aid programs, including the Departments of Treasury (e.g., providing advice on taxes or fiscal policies) and Justice (providing help on strengthening the judiciaries in foreign countries). Additionally, the Treasury takes the lead in providing debt relief for developing countries, appropriated at $123 million in fiscal year 2000. The aid programs of these two agencies fall primarily into the categories of economic development and democratization, respectively. However, some of the overseas activities that these departments fund also support economic and political transitions in former socialist bloc countries.

The Departments of Transportation, Agriculture, Commerce, Labor, Interior, Energy, and Health and Human Services and the Environmental Protection Agency also have foreign aid programs, falling primarily into the category of addressing transnational issues. Some of the activities of these agencies are funded from USAID's budget. Others come directly from funds appropriated to the agencies themselves. Finally, the Departments of State and Defense fund concessional expenditures abroad in the areas of humanitarian relief.

Multilateral Development Banks

There are seven multilateral development banks—the World Bank and regional banks for Latin America, Asia, Africa, Europe, and North America and the Middle East.

The *World Bank* is the oldest and largest multilateral development bank. Its primary purpose is to promote economic and social development, through concessional loans to governments of poor countries and with "hard" loans (at near-commercial rates) to governments of better-off developing countries. Some of its lending has also supported economic transitions in former socialist countries. A small amount of funding has been provided recently for humanitarian relief, war-to-peace transition, and people-centered development activities undertaken by NGOs. Its overall annual lending level in 1999 (in commitments) was $29 billion. Within this overall level, concessional loans to poor countries amounted to $6.8 billion.

The *Inter-American Development Bank* provides soft and hard loans to governments of the countries of Central and South America and the Caribbean. Most of these loans fall into the category of economic development, although it tends to put more emphasis on social issues in its region than the World Bank does. The total level of lending was over $10 billion in 1998. The *Asian Development Bank and Fund* makes loans to the governments of its 40 member countries, located in Central, South, and East Asia. It lent $5 billion in 1999, and provided technical assistance grants of nearly $135 million. Most of the projects and programs funded by it fall into the category of economic development, as described above. The *African Development Bank and Fund* provides loans—mainly highly concessional ones—to its 53 African member states in North and Sub-Saharan Africa in support of economic development. Its total lending amounted to nearly $2 billion in 1998. This institution has been the most troubled of the regional development banks. It has had a difficult time finding a niche for itself in funding development in Africa, has suffered in the past from poor management and corruption, and faces problems of nonperforming loans to many of its borrowers.

The *European Bank for Reconstruction and Development* was set up in 1991 to promote the economic transition from socialist to free-market economies in former socialist countries. It loaned over $2 billion in 1999 in 25 countries.

The *North American Development Bank* (NADBank), established as part of the North American Free Trade Area (NAFTA) in 1993, makes loans and leverages private investment for infrastructure (particularly in the area of environment) in communities in the border area between the United States and Mexico and in communities hurt by NAFTA. The United States contributed $56.5 million to the NADBank in 1998.

The *Economic Cooperation and Development Bank for the Middle East and North Africa*, proposed by the United States in 1994 to promote the Middle East peace process and encourage greater investment and cooperation in the region, has yet to be established and funded. The Clinton administration proposed a US contribution to this bank of $52 million in 1998. Though Congress provided no funding for this bank in 1997 or 1998, it continues to have the support of the administration.

International Organizations and Programs

The United States contributes to the funding of more than 70 international organizations and programs working in the area of development, humanitarian relief, and transnational issues.[1] Most of these organiza-

---

1. US contributions are either assessed—i.e., the US share of an overall agency budget that the United States as a member is obligated to provide—or they are voluntary—the level of contribution is decided by the US government. Although most data on US foreign aid exclude assessed contributions, the figures on funding in this section include both. The number of international organizations and programs working in development is based on a report by the US General Accounting Office that lists all the international organizations and programs to which the US government contributed in 1995. Those organizations whose work fits the definition of development for the purposes of this study are included here. Descriptions of the organizations with the amounts of

tions and programs are associated with the United Nations, either as UN programs or as specialized agencies. Many of them—27 to be exact—are quite small, with total US contributions annually of $1 million or less. We shall not examine all of the smaller organizations here.

Many of these international organizations and programs were set up to promote multilateral cooperation on particular issues, often falling into the category of purposes we have termed transnational issues, such as health, food and agriculture, or the environment. A number of them provide humanitarian relief, whereas several others provide assistance for economic development. One provides funding to promote democracy in the Western Hemisphere.

Development Organizations and Programs

The two largest recipients of US aid in this group are the *United Nations Development Program* (UNDP) and the *United Nations Children's Fund* (UNICEF), to which the United States contributed $98 and $100 million respectively in 1998.[2] UNDP documents emphasize the perspective of social development, but much of its funding—which is channeled to governments or other UN agencies—is used to finance technical assistance largely focused on traditional economic development activities and transnational issues. UNICEF's activities, focused on improving the lives of children, fall into the category of humane concerns.

The *International Fund for Agricultural Development* (not part of the United Nations), providing aid for small holder agriculture, also fits into the category of economic development. It received $2.5 million from the United States in 1998.

International Humanitarian Organizations and Programs

The two main international organizations in this category are the *UN High Commissioner for Refugees* (UNHCR) and the *World Food Program* (WFP). UNHCR provides assistance to refugees and displaced people. Its budget (and the US contribution to it) varies according to the number of refugees it serves. In 1998, it had a total budget of just under $1 billion. The WFP provides food to victims of natural and man-made disasters (including both refugees and displaced people). It also provides food in

---

US contributions and the US government agencies making those contributions are included in the appendix. See General Accounting Office, *Multilateral Organizations: U.S. Contributions to International Organizations for Fiscal Years 1993-95*, GAO/NSIAD-97-42 (Washington, May 1997).

2. These are planned voluntary contributions. It is often the case that additional monies are allocated to these organizations by USAID and other government agencies. I do not have data on any additional allocations from the US government.

support of development projects, for example, offering food to laborers in public works projects as payment for labor. Its total budget for 1997 was $1.2 billion, with contributions from the United States totaling $375 million.

Transnational Issues

Many UN agencies, regional organizations, and other multilateral institutions were set up initially to address what we now term transnational issues, including population, food, health, and the environment. The *UN Population Fund* (UNFPA) is charged with expanding the use of family planning worldwide. It received $30 million from the United States in 1998.

In agriculture, the United States supports the *Food and Agriculture Organization* (FAO), which gathers information on and monitors agricultural production worldwide, provides technical assistance, and funds projects in agriculture for a number of countries throughout the world. The United States (assessed) contribution to the FAO in 1998 was $80.8 million.

Another multilateral organization, with an unusual informal structure is the *Consultative Group on International Agricultural Research* (CGIAR). This organization is responsible for a wide range of research on agricultural products and related policy and issues. It is a network of 16 international research institutes and received $38 million from the United States in 1999.

The *Inter-American Institute for Cooperation on Agriculture*, a specialized agency of the Organization of American States, gathers information and provides technical assistance and training on agriculture in the Western Hemisphere. The US contribution to this agency was $17 million in 1998.

On international health issues, the principal international health organization is the *World Health Organization* (WHO), a UN agency that gathers data and promotes research and technical assistance on a wide range of international health issues. The US contribution to WHO in 1998 was $107 million from the Department of State budget (assessed), with another $30 million or more added on a voluntary basis from USAID and other US government agencies.

The *Pan American Health Organization* (PAHO) is a separate organization from WHO but serves as its regional office in the Western Hemisphere and fulfills similar functions. The US contribution to PAHO in 1998 was $50 million.

Since the mid-1990s, international environmental issues have been a growth area for international organizations and programs. The larger ones (to which the United States contributes $3 million or more per year) are the *UN Environment Program* (UNEP), the *Montreal Protocol Fund*, the *Global Environment Facility* (GEF), and the *Convention on International Trade in Endangered Species of Wild Fauna and Flora* (CITES).

UNEP gathers data on international environmental issues, sponsors negotiations on environmental problems, encourages research, and acts as a secretariat for several international agreements, such as the Convention on Biodiversity. It also provides technical assistance to governments on environmental issues. The United States contributed $11 million to UNEP in 1998. In the same year, it also provided $5 million in support of the International Panel on Climate Change, which is housed in UNEP.

The Montreal Protocol Fund grew out of the Montreal Protocol on Substances that Deplete the Ozone Layer, signed by major industrial countries in 1987. Its role is to help developing countries finance the cost of eliminating the use of ozone-depleting chemicals. The United States contributed $28 million to it in 1998.

The GEF was set up in 1990 to finance activities in developing countries addressing four areas of environmental concern—global warming, protecting biodiversity, decreasing ozone layer depletion, and protecting international waters. After the UN Conference on the Environment and Development in Rio de Janeiro in 1992, the GEF began to fund activities in the area of biodiversity and climate change. In 1998, the United States contribution to the GEF was $100 million.

CITES, signed in 1975, regulates trade in such commodities as elephant tusks as a means of discouraging the destruction of endangered wild animals and plants. In 1998, the United States contributed $3.7 million to CITES, the International Union for the Conservation of Nature, and several other international organizations involved with conservation.

Finally, with regard to the promotion of democracy, the *Organization of American States Development Assistance Program* promotes programs encouraging democratic participation in Latin American countries. The United States contributed $6.5 million to this program in 1998.

Appendix B: Assumptions and Estimates for Aid Matrix

The estimates of funding falling into these categories are no more than broadly indicative of the magnitudes of funds due to the limitations of the data and the fact that agencies do not collect and present budgetary data in these particular categories.

I have made a number of assumptions regarding the funding estimates. For security purposes, I have included all $2.4 billion in ESF monies, nearly all of which were spent in the Middle East, Cyprus, Northern Ireland and Haiti. For economic development and humane concerns, I have included $1.3 billion in US contributions for multilateral development banks (except those to the European Bank for Reconstruction and Development and NADBank, and funding for the GEF, which I have included in transnational issues). I have also included US contribution to the UNDP ($98 million), International Fund for Agricultural Development ($2.5 million) and all PL 480 Title III (food aid) funds ($30 million, provided in support of policy reform programs). Additionally, the administration spent $27 million to finance the cancellation of debts owed the US government.

To estimate the amount of Development Assistance funds that were allocated to economic development in 1998 (an admittedly highly speculative exercise because USAID does not keep its data in the categories used here), I have taken the total amount of Development Assistance allocated to countries and regions ($1.3 billion) and have subtracted funding for democracy programs (approximately $120 million). Thus, the total for development—including expenditures by USAID and US contributions to multilateral development banks and international organizations—is $3.4 billion (on the basis of 1998 data).

Funding for humanitarian relief, including war-to-peace transitions, includes $190 million from USAID in disaster assistance, $332 million in food aid (managed by USAID's central bureaus for emergency purposes), $69 million in additional "humanitarian response" funds by USAID, and $700 million in funding for refugees overseas provided by the Department of State.

Monies for economic and political transitions in Eastern Europe and the former USSR from the European Bank for Reconstruction and Development plus US bilateral funding for the same region (managed by USAID) total $1.5 billion.

Funding for addressing transnational issues includes $300 million from USAID's Bureau for Global Affairs dedicated to addressing these issues, including US voluntary contributions in 1998 to UNFPA, FAO, the Inter-American Institute for Cooperation on Agriculture, WHO, PAHO, UNEP, the Montreal Fund, GEF, CITES, and NADBank, totaling $400 million. Funding for democracy includes $120 million from USAID's Development Assistance monies, $10 million from ESF, and $30 million for the National Endowment for Democracy.

Index

AARP, 50n
abortion issue, 46
Afghanistan, 59, 63
AFL-CIO (American Federation of Labor—
    Congress of Industrial Organizations),
    51
Africa
    AIDS, 75
    conflicts, 59, 60, 61
    life expectancy, 75
    priority status, 40-41
    projected population, 62t
    trends in aid, 14
    urbanization, 65
    water issues, 67
African Development Bank and Fund, 32t,
    99
African Development Foundation, 32t
    aid amounts, 11t
    bilateral aid, 10, 42
    described, 97-98
    future planning, 92
agribusiness enterprises, 71
agriculture
    Consultative Group on International
        Agricultural Research (CGIAR), 32t,
        70, 71, 101
    InterAmerican Institute for Cooperation on
        Agriculture, 32t, 101
    International Fund for Agricultural
        Development, 100
    international regime, 70-71
    research and development, 51, 69, 70-71
    water demand, 66
Agriculture Department, 12, 26

AIDS
    Africa, 75
    orphans, 20, 21
AIPAC (American Israel Public Affairs
    Committee), 50-51, 50n
Albright, Madeleine, 40
Algeria, 59
Alliance for Progress, 18n
Amarasinghe, Upali, 67n
American Israel Public Affairs Committee
    (AIPAC), 50-51, 50n
amounts of US aid, 33-34
Anderson, J. Brady, 22n
Anderson, Mary B., 25n
Angola, 59, 61
anticommunism, 18
appropriations bills, 45-46
appropriations committees, 37, 38
    decision making, 38
appropriations process, 39-40
authorization committees, 38-39
appropriations subcommittees, 45
Argentina, 64n
Armenia, 51
    conflicts, 61
    income distribution, 63
    political and economic transitions, 25
Arms Control and Disarmament Agency, 41
Asia
    domestic savings and investment, 82
    energy issues, 71
    foreign aid as diplomatic tool, 40
    poverty, 82, 83
    projected population, 62t
    water issues, 67

Asia Foundation, 11
Asian Development Bank and Fund, 32*t*
    aid amounts, 11*t*
    described, 98-99
Asian financial crisis, 64, 77-78
associational revolution, 85
Atwood, J. Brian, 43*n*
authoritarian regimes, 26, 83
authorization process, Congress, 38-39
Azerbaijan
    conflicts, 61
    incomes, 63
    political and economic transitions, 25

Balkans, 61
Ball, Nicole, 23*n*
Barker, Randolph, 57*n*
Barry, Robert, 2, 3*n*
Battle of Seattle, 79, 80
bilateral aid
    African Development Foundation, 42
    amounts, 11*t*
    contest for control, 41
    deconcentrated, 29
    division of labor, 91
    focus, 31
    food supply, 70
    future purposes, 91, 92
    InterAmerican Foundation, 42
    management of, 5
    multilateral agencies versus, 43
    need to reconfigure, 5
    new collaborations, 5
    organizations described, 97-98
    organizations listed, 32*t*
    Peace Corps, 42-43
    State Department control, 40, 41
binational commissions, 13-14
bio-terrorism, 13
biodiversity, 74, 102
Birnbaum, Jeffrey H., 50*n*
Bosnia, aid levels, 29
Brazil, 64*n*
Brown, Lester, 69*n*
Buchanan-Smith, Margaret, 23*n*
budgetary levels, 6
    trends in aid, 14-15, 14*f*
budgetary process, 35-38
    "150" account, 37*n*
    deficits and offsets, 39
    public perceptions, 53
Burundi, 59

Cambodia, 59, 61, 63, 67
Camp David Accords, 18
Canada, 15, 69
capital flight, 78
capital flows, 82
    private, 64

short-term volatility, 78-79
    trade, 77
Caribbean
    bilateral aid, 29
    economic growth, 78*t*
    foreign direct investment, 77*t*
Carothers, Thomas, 26*n*
Center for Disease Control (Atlanta), 75
Center for International Labor Solidarity, 51
Center for Strategic and International Studies, 2
Central America
    disaster assistance, 15
    Reagan foreign policy, 46
Central Asia
    income distribution, 63
    political and economic transitions, 25, 84
Central Europe, political and economic transitions, 84
Chase, Robert, 2, 3*n*
child survival issue, 20
Chile, 26, 64*n*
children
    aid to commercial interests, 47
    child survival and disease programs, 20, 48*t*
    congressional aid preferences, 48
    congressional support, 54-55
    future policy, 85
    humane concerns, 20
    new rationale, 48
China
    FDI, 64*n*
    poverty, 64
    water issues, 67
cholera, 75, 76
Christopher, Warren, 41
Cilluffo, Frank, 80*n*
citizen participation, 58
civil conflicts, 22, 59
civil society, limitations, 83
Clinton, Pres. William J., binational commissions, 13-14
Club du Sahel, 65*n*
Codex Alimentarius, 70
Cold War, security issues, 18-19
Colombia, 59
    conflicts, 59
    Plan Colombia, 11, 15
Commerce Department, 11, 44-45
communications technology, 85
community service organizations, 51
complex crises, 22
concessional resource transfers, 9
conflicts
    civil, 22, 59, 60-61
    conflict reduction, 26
    defined, 58*n*
    interstate, 59-60
    intrastate, 59-60
    water issues, 67

Congress, 40-45
   appropriations committees, 37, 38
   appropriations process, 39-40
   authorization process, 38-39
   budget from president, 36-37
   budgetary process, 36-39
   child aid, 54-55
   Congressional Presentations, 37
   consensus on foreign aid, 37
   constituent skepticism, 49
   lobbying other members, 48-49
   public opinion, 54
   transforming foreign aid, 95
   voting motivations, 48
Congressional Quarterly, 48n
Consultative Group on International
   Agricultural Research (CGIAR), 32t, 70,
   71, 101
contagion fears, 78
continuing resolutions, 36, 38, 45
Convention on Biodiversity, 102
Convention on International Trade in
   Endangered Species of Wild Fauna and
   Flora (CITES), 32t
   description, 71, 101, 102
   funding, 71
coordination problem, 90, 90n
   interagency coordination, 93-94
Council on Foreign Relations, 79n
country programming model, 28, 29-30
crisis prevention, 28
Cuba, 84
Czech Republic, 25

DAC (Development Assistance Committee of
   OECD), 9
   membership, 15n
debt relief, 98
   amounts, 11t
Defense Department
   concessional expenditures abroad, 12
   humanitarian emergencies, 30, 34, 98
democracy promotion, 25-26
   Alliance for Progress, 18n
   foreign aid matrix, 33t, 103
   as future priority, 86
   future prospects, 83-84
   international organizations, 100
   Justice Department, 98
   OAS Development Assistance Program, 32t,
   102
   purposes of foreign aid, 19-21
Democratic Republic of the Congo, 59
democratization, 3, 98
Destler, I.M., 53n, 54, 54n
development agencies, 90
Development Assistance
   amount, 11t, 15, 16f
   as bilateral aid, 10

foreign aid matrix, 33t, 103
   nongovernmental organizations (NGOs)
     funded, 10
   State Department, 40
   USAID management, 41
Development Assistance Committee of OECD.
   see DAC
development rationale, 55
disaster assistance
   Central America, 15
   humanitarian relief, 21-25
   Kosovo, 15
   Office of Foreign Disaster Assistance, 24
disease
   new rationale, 48
   urbanization, 75
displaced people and refugees, 59
drug resistance, 75
drug trade, 80-81
drugs, for disease control, 76

Eagleburger, Lawrence, 2, 3n
earmarks, congressional, 48, 51
East Asia
   economic growth, 78t
   foreign direct investment, 77t
East West Institute, 11
Eastern Europe
   aid amounts, 11t, 103
   political and economic transitions, 25, 84
   SEED/NIS, 33t
   trends in aid, 14
economic assistance, 46
   rationale weakened, 47-48
Economic Cooperation and Development Bank
   for the Middle East and North Africa,
   32t, 99
economic development
   development agencies, 90
   development organizations and programs,
   100
   development rationale weakened, 47-48
   foreign aid matrix, 33t, 102
   future prospects, 82-83, 86, 91
   humane concerns, 20
   purposes of foreign aid, 19-21
   State Department, 40
   three approaches to aid, 20-21
   transnational issues, 20
   Treasury Department, 98
economic growth
   aid for, 19
   developing nations, 64, 78t
Economic Support Fund (ESF)
   amounts, 11t
   as bilateral aid, 10
   foreign aid matrix, 33t, 102
   predecessor, 18
   State Department role, 40

Economic Support Fund (ESF) (*Cont.*):
  trends in aid, 14
  USAID management, 41
economic transitions, 25
  foreign aid matrix, 33*t*, 34
education, developing countries, 63
Egypt
  aid levels, 29
  bilateral aid, 33-34
  binational commissions, 13-14
  peacemaking focus, 18
El Salvador, 64
end of the Cold War
  new aid programs, 13
  security threat shift, 86
  US strategic concerns, 40
endangered species. *See* Convention on
    International Trade in Endangered
    Species of Wild Fauna and Flora
    (CITES)
Energy Department, 12, 71*n*, 72*n*
  international regime, 72
energy issues, 71-72
  demand, 71-72
  international regime, 72
  supply, 72
Engleman, Robert, 67*n*
environmental issues, 66
  international regime, 73-74
  organizations, 51, 101-02
  problems described, 72-73
  scarcity issues, 66-72
Environmental Protection Agency (EPA),
    foreign assistance programs, 12, 13
Eritrea, 59
ESF. *See* Economic Support Fund (ESF)
Estonia, political and economic transitions, 25,
    84
Ethiopia, 59
Europe
  projected population, 62*t*
  water issues, 67
European Bank for Reconstruction and
    Development, 32*t*
  aid amounts, 11*t*
  described, 99
  foreign aid matrix, 33*t*
Exchange Stabilization Fund, 81
Executive Branch, 39-45
  as advocate, 54
  announcement of policy, 35
  appropriations bills signing, 39
  budget to Congress, 36-37
  Department of State, 39-41
  diminishing interest in foreign aid, 44
  lobbying Congress, 49
  OMB, 43
  public opinion, 54
  Treasury, 43
  unexpected contingencies, 39

USAID, 31-32
  White House, 44-45
export promotion, 27-28
Export-Import Bank, 44-45

faith-based organizations, 51
family planning, 18*n*
  abortion issue, 46
  organizations, 51
  UN Population Fund, 32*t*, 101
Farber, Henry S., 26*n*
Fascel, Dante, 43*n*
field missions, 29
financial crisis
  Asian financial crisis, 64, 77-78
  short-term volatility, 78-79, 81
Flavin, Christopher, 69*n*
Food and Agriculture Organization (FAO),
    32*t*, 69*n*, 70
  described, 101
food aid, 10
  amounts, 11*t*
  farmer constituency, 41
  foreign aid matrix, 33*t*, 34
  USAID management, 41
food issues, 69-71
  basic research, 71
  future demand, 69
  future supply, 69-70
  genetically engineered crops, 71
  urbanization, 65-66
  World Food Program (WFP), 100-101
foreign aid
  aid effectiveness, 6*n*
  amounts in 1986-2000 period, 14*f*
  concept of, 9
  forms of, 10
  four future purposes, 84-87
  purposes, 17-25
  for future, 4-5
  shifting priorities, 4
foreign aid matrix, 33-34, 102-03
foreign direct investment (FDI), 15, 64
  developing world by region, 77*t*
foreign governments, 53
Foreign Office (FO), 90*n*
foreign operations subcommittees, 37
  earmarks for constituents, 48
foreign policy, foreign aid as, 46
fossil fuels, 72
foundation model, 28, 30
foundations, 5
  funding, 11
France, aid levels, 15
French, Hilary, 69*n*

Gardner-Outlaw, Tom, 67*n*
General Accounting Office (GAO), 100*n*

genetically engineered crops, 71
Georgia
    conflicts, 61
    political and economic transitions, 25
Germany
    aid levels, 15
    development agency, 90n
Ghana, 64
Gleick, Peter, 67n
global commons, 66
Global Environment Facility, 32t, 74, 101,
    102
global warming, 102
Global Water Partnership, 68-69
globalization, 76-81
    benefits and costs, 77-78
    of government agencies, 5
    losers in, 79-81
    negative consequences, 4
    transnational problems increasing, 20-21
Goldstein, Morris, 78n
Gordon, David, 1, 3n
Gore, Albert, 41, 44
governance focus, 31
government agencies
    among organizations funded, 32t
    coordination problem, 90-91
    foreign aid politics, 37n
    foreign aid programs, 12
    foreign aid programs described, 98
    funding, 12
    future prospects, 93
    interagency coordination, 93-94
    Russia, aid to, 45n
    shutdown, 45
    transnational issues, 21
Gowa, Joanne, 26n
Graham, Carol, 2, 3n
Greece, 51
greenhouse effect, International Panel on
    Climate Change, 102
Gruebler, A., 71n
Grunberg, Isabelle, 3, 3n; 20n, 62n
Guinea-Bissau, 59
Gwin, Catherine, 1, 3n, 19n

Haas, Peter M., 74n
Haiti, 29, 63
Harvard Institute for International
    Development, 52
Health and Human Services (HHS)
    Department, 12
    WHO role, 12
health issues, 86
    Pan American Health Organization
        (PAHO), 32t, 101
    World Health Organization (WHO), 12, 32t,
        76, 91, 101
    see also disease; HIV/AIDS

Helms, Jesse, 41
Henning, C. Randall, 81n
Hill, Emily, 3
HIV/AIDS
    new rationale, 48
    orphans, 20, 21
Honduras, 63
House International Relations Committee, 37
Hufbauer, Gary, 80, 80n
humane concerns, 4
    economic development, 20
    funding, 33t, 34
    future policy, 85, 92
    sustainable policy, 87
humanitarian relief, 4, 21-25
    challenges ahead, 86-87
    complex crises, 22
    Defense Department, 30, 34, 98
    foreign aid matrix, 33t, 102, 103
    foreign policy goals, 87
    new paradigm, 55
    organizations and programs described, 100-
        101
    policy shift, 22, 92
    purposes, of foreign aid, 21-25
    rapid response management, 30
    State Department, 98
humanitarian-oriented organizations, 51-52
Humphrey, Hubert, 48
Hungary, political and economic transitions,
    25

immigrants, 50
income distribution, 63, 79n
India, 59, 64n
    disease, 75
    poverty, 64
    water issues, 67
Indochina, war in, 46
Indonesia, 59, 61, 64n
    capital flight, 78
infectious disease, 4
    congressional initiative, 21
    current challenges, 74-76
information technology, 3
infrastructure projects, 47n
integration, 90-91n
Inter-American Development Bank, 32t, 98
Inter-American Development and Investment
    Corporation, aid amounts, 11t
InterAction, 51
interagency coordination, 93-94
InterAmerican Foundation, 32t
    as bilateral aid, 10
    bilateral aid, 42
    described, 97-98
    foundation model, 28, 30
    future planning, 92
    support, 43n

InterAmerican Institute for Cooperation on Agriculture, 32t, 101
interest-group politics, 52-53
Interior Department, 12
International Conference on Water and the Environment, 68n
International Energy Agency, 72
International Food Policy Research Institute, 69
International Fund for Agricultural Development, 32t, 70, 100, 102
International Labor Organization (ILO), 12
International Monetary Fund (IMF)
  economic policy reform, 31
  studies of, 2
  volatility of capital flows, 79, 81
international organizations, 53
  aid amounts, 11t
  budgetary process, 36
  described, 99-100
  early 21st century projections, 57
  leadership selection, 91-92
  organizations listed, 32t
  US contributions, 99-100n
International Panel on Climate Change, 102
international public goods, 3, 62n
  see also transnational issues
International Water Management Institute, 69
Internet, 85
interstate conflicts, 59-60
intrastate conflicts, 59-60
Iran, 59
Iraq, 59
Israel
  aid levels, 29
  conflicts, 59
  effectiveness of organizations, 55
  peacemaking focus, 18
  support, 50
  water issues, 67
  Wye River Agreement, 15, 18
Italy, aid levels, 15

Japan
  as largest donor, 15
  prosperity, 63
Javits, Jacob, 48
Jordan, 67
Justice Department, 12, 98

Kanbur, Ravi, 3, 3n, 20n, 62n
Kaplan, Robert, 59, 59n
Kaul, Inge, 3, 3n, 20n, 62n
Kazakhstan
  binational commissions, 13-14
  political and economic transitions, 25
Keck, Margaret, 86n

Kennedy, Paul, 2, 3n
Keohane, Robert O., 74n
Kosovo, disaster assistance, 15
Kull, Steven, 53n, 54, 54n
Kumar, Krishna, 23n
Kyrgys Republic, 63

Labor Department, 12
  ILO representation, 12
labor movement, 51
  National Endowment for Democracy, 11, 26
Lake, Anthony, 26, 26n
Lancaster, Carol, 6n, 65n, 90n
Laos, 63
Latin America
  Asian financial crisis, 78
  bilateral aid, 29
  cholera, 75
  democracy promotion, 102
  domestic savings and investment, 82
  economic growth, 78t
  foreign aid as diplomatic tool, 40
  foreign direct investment, 77t
  income distribution, 63
  poverty, 82-83
  projected population, 62t
Leach, James, 46n
Levy, Marc A., 74n
liberalization of trade, 79, 79n
lobbying
  foreign governments, 53
  international organizations, 53
  private groups, 52-53

McDonald, A., 71n
Malaysia, 64n
management of US foreign aid, 28-31
  principal models, 28-31
  country programming model, 28, 29-30
  foundation model, 28, 30
  opportunistic model, 28-29
  rapid response model, 30
Mansfield, Edward D., 26n
market economies, 26
  short-term volatility, 78
matrix, foreign aid, 33-34, 102-03
Maxwell, Simon, 23n
Medicins sans Frontiers, 25n
Mexico, 64n
micro-enterprise lending, 51
Middle East, 40
  conflicts, 59, 60
  economic growth, 78t
  effectiveness of organizations, 55
  foreign direct investment, 77t
  income distribution, 63
  water issues, 67
migration, 75

military assistance, 46, 47
Plan Colombia, 11, 15
ministries of foreign affairs, 90
mission creep, 5
mixed credits, 27
Mongolia, 63
Montreal Protocol Fund, 32t, 101, 102
Montreal Protocol on Ozone Depletion, 74, 102
Morrison, Kevin M., 3n, 20n, 62n
multilateral aid
Congress, 37
division of labor with bilateral aid, 91
organizations listed, 32t
multilateral development banks (MDBs)
bilateral aid as, 43
budgetary process, 36
described, 98-99
division of labor, 91
Treasury Department, 43
Myanmar, 59, 63

Nakkenovic, N., 71n
National Endowment for Democracy, 11, 26
National Security Council, 42, 43
Nelson, Ivan, 19n
Netherlands, 68, 68n, 69
Nicaragua, 14, 63
nonconcessional lending, 82-83
nongovernmental organizations (NGOs), 5
activism, 85
associational revolution, 85
civil society and democracy, 26
Development Assistance fund, 10
early 21st century organizations, 57
foundation management model, 30
percentage of aid, 20
relief and recovery assistance, 24
transforming foreign aid, 95
umbrella organization, 51
North Africa, 67
economic growth, 78t
foreign direct investment, 77t
North American Development Bank, 32t, 99
North American Free Trade Agreement
(NAFTA), 99
North Korea, 24
economic growth under authoritarian
regimes, 26
North South Institute, 11
Northern America, projected population, 62t
Norway, 15
NSC. See National Security Council

Oceania, projected population, 62t
OECD (Organization for Economic Cooperation and Development), 23n, 77n
defining foreign aid, 9
Development Assistance Committee, 9

Office of Foreign Disaster Assistance (OFDA),
24, 30
Office of Management and Budget (OMB),
12n
as actor in politics of foreign aid, 43
budgetary process, 36, 36t
NSC versus, 43
role, 43
State Department versus, 43
offsetting reductions, 39
O'Hanlon, Michael, 2
oil supplies, 72
omnibus spending bills, 38, 45
opportunistic model, 28-29
Organization of American States (OAS)
agricultural training, 32t, 101
Development Assistance Program, 32t,
102
organization of foreign aid, 31-32
brief description of organizations, 97-102
future, 89-94
overlapping functions, 31-32
Overseas Development Council (ODC), 1, 52
ozone depletion, 73, 74, 102

Pacific
economic growth, 78t
foreign direct investment, 77t
Pakistan, 59, 67
Palestine, Wye River Agreement, 15, 18
Pan American Health Organization (PAHO),
32t, 101
Panama, 14
Pandya-lorch, Rajul, 69n
Peace Corps, 32t
aid amounts, 11t
bilateral aid, 42-43
described, 97
independence, 92
peacemaking
Cold War era, 18
consensus lacking, 89
future policy, 86
United States as superpower, 4
Wye River Agreement, 18
people of concern, 60t
Peru, 59, 75, 76
pharmaceutical companies, 5
Philippines, 59
Pinstrup-Anderson, 66n, 69n
pivotal states, 2
Plan Colombia, 11, 15
Poland
FDI, 64n
political and economic transitions, 25
policy paradigm, for foreign aid, 4-5, 89
political environment, 46, 49
political parties, 46-47
democratic facade, 83

political reform, 26
political and social reconstruction, 23-24
political transitions, 25
    democracy promotion efforts, 84
    foreign aid matrix, 33*t*
    Portugal, 18*n*
politics of foreign aid, 35-55
    actors, 39-54
        Congress, 40-45
        Executive Branch, 39-40
        foreign governments and international
            organizations, 53
        interests versus values, 89
        private groups, 50-53
        public opinion, 53-54
    appropriations process, 35-38
    budgetary process, 35-38
poor nations
    basic agricultural research, 71
    conflict levels, 59
    development rationale, 47-48
    economic development, 19
    economic development aid, 82-83
    food supply, 70
    future aid, 91
    health systems, 75-76
    humanitarian intervention, 21-22
    ozone depletion, 74
    partisan interests, 47
    population, 62, 63
    US exports, 27-28
    water issues, 67
    world conditions, 64-65
population
    growth, 62-63, 62*t*
    programs, 18n
    projected, 62*t*
    as transnational issues, 62-63
    UN Population Fund, 32*t*, 101
    urban, 65
    water demand, 66
Portugal, political transitions, 18*n*
poverty
    Asia, 82
    Latin America, 82-83
    world conditions, 64-65
presidents, diminishing interest in
        foreign aid, 44
preventive diplomacy, 28
private organizations, 50-53
    lobbying, 52-53
    USAID support, 42
private sector, financial flows, 16
private/corporate enterprises, 5
    early 21st century projections, 57
    foundation management model, 30
proliferation of functions, 2
prosperity/poverty, 63-65
public administration, 89-90
public health challenges, 86

Public Law 480 (PL 480)
    as bilateral aid, 10
    Department of Agriculture, 34
    funding, 103
    USAID management, 41
public opinion, 53-54, 93
    public pressure, 52-53
purposes, of foreign aid, 17-25
    congressional influence, 47-50
    democracy promotion, 256
    four future purposes, 84-87
    humanitarian relief, 21-25
    other rationales, 27-28
        export promotion, 27-28
        preventing conflict, 28
    political and economic transitions, 25
    promoting development, 19-21
    promoting security, 18-19

Raine, Linnea, 80*n*
rapid response model, 30
Rees, Susan, 50*n*
refugees, 59, 60*t*
regime transitions. *See* political transitions
regional development banks, focus, 31
relief aid
    future challenges, 87
    humanitarian, 21-25
    refugees, 60*t*
renewable energy sources, 72
Rodrik, Dani, 79*n*
Romania, political and economic transitions,
        25
Rosegrant, Mark, 66*n*, 67*n*, 69*n*
rule of law, 77
Russia
    aid levels, 29
    binational commissions, 13-14
    disease, 75
    political and economic transitions, 25, 84
    USAID, 45*n*
Ruttan, Vernon, 1-2, 3*n*
Rwanda, 24-25*n*, 59, 61, 87

safety net, international, 81
Salamon, Lester, 85*n*
Sandler, Todd, 3, 3*n*, 62*n*
scarcity issues, 66-72
    energy, 71-72
    food, 69-71
    water, 66-69
Seattle WTO meeting, 79, 80
Seckler, David, 67*n*
Secretary General, United Nations, 65*n*
security issues
    foreign aid matrix, 33*t*
    future policy, 86
    purposes of foreign aid, 18-19
    rationale after Cold War, 47, 55

Sen, Amartya, 20*n*
Senate Foreign Relations Committee, 37-38
Serageldin, Ismael, 68*n*
Sierra Leone, 59
Sikkink, Kathryn, 86*n*
Sinding, Steve, 1, 3*n*
Slovenia, political and economic transitions, 25
Smillie, Ian, 23*n*
Snyder, Jack, 26*n*
Sollenberg, Margareta, 58*n*
South Africa, binational commissions, 13-14
South Asia
  economic growth, 78*t*
  foreign direct investment, 77*t*
South Korea, capital flight, 78
Southeast Asia, income distribution, 63
Soviet Union, former, 103
  economic growth, 64
Spiro, David, 26*n*
Sri Lanka, 59, 64
State Department
  as actor in politics of foreign aid, 39-41
  Bureau of Political Military Affairs, 92
  civil society, 26
  concessional expenditures abroad, 12
  ESF role, 40
  formerly socialist nations, 25
  Global Affairs Bureau, 92
  humanitarian relief, 98
  merger with USAID, 41, 41*n*
  Office of Plans, Programs and Budgets,
    92
  OMB versus, 43
  program management critiqued, 92-93
  refugee programs, 11*t*, 92
  relief and transition assistance, 24
  reorganizing, 92-93
  undersecretary for global issues, 21
Stern, Marc A., 3, 3*n*, 20*n*, 62*n*
strategic threats, 28
street children, 20
Sub-Saharan Africa, 40
  capital flows and trade, 80
  economic growth, 78*t*
  education, 63
  food supply, 70
  foreign direct investment, 77*t*
  income distribution, 63
  population growth, 62
  poverty, 64-65, 83
Sudan, 59, 87
Sweden, 69
Swedish International peace Research Institute
    (SIPRI), 58-59, 58*n*, 59*n*
Syria, 67

Taiwan, 26
Tajikistan, 61, 63
terrorism, 80-81

Thailand, 78
think tanks, 50, 52
trade and investment, 44-45
  drug trade, 80-81
  liberalization, 79
transnational issues, 61-76
  agencies described, 101-02
  challenge, 4
  economic development, 20
  energy problem, 72
  externalities, 72-76
  foreign aid matrix, 33*t*, 34
  future policy, 86
  globalization effects, 20-21
  international organizations, 91
  international organizations and programs,
    100
  new paradigm, 55
  population, 62-63
  prosperity/poverty, 63-65
  scarcity issues, 66-72
  urbanization, 65-66
  USAID-State merger, 41
Transportation Department, 12
Treasury, Department of the
  as actor in politics of foreign aid, 43
  financial crises, 81
  foreign aid programs described, 98
  foreign assistance programs, 12
  functions, 34
trends in US aid, 14-15, 14*f*
tuberculosis, 48, 75
Turkey, 59, 67
Turkmenistan, 63

Uganda, 29, 59
Ukraine
  aid levels, 29
  binational commissions, 13-14
  disease, 75
  political and economic transitions, 25,
    84
UN Children's Fund, 32*t*, 100
UN Commission on Sustainable
    Development, 73
UN Conference on the Environment and
    Development, 73, 102
UN Development Program (UNDP), 32*t*
  described, 100
  field mission, 29
  funding, 102
  research, 3, 3*n*
  water issues, 68
UN Environment Program (UNEP), 32*t*, 73,
    101-02
UN High Commissioner for Refugees, 32*t*,
    60*t*, 100
UN Population Fund, 32*t*, 101
UN Water Conference of 1977, 68*n*

United Kingdom
  aid levels, 15
  development agency, 90*n*
  think tanks, 52
United Nations
  leadership selection, 91
  programs described, 100
  water issues, 68*n*
United States
  aid levels comparatively, 15
  disease, 75
  early 21st century projections, 57-58
universities
  agricultural research and development, 51
  foreign aid research, 52
  Harvard Institute for International
    Development, 52
urbanization, 65-66
  disease, 75
US Information Agency, 41
USAID (US Agency for International
    Development), 27*n*, 28*n*, 32*t*
  as actor in politics of foreign aid, 39-41
  Bureau of Global Issues, 21, 103
  civil society, 26
  described, 97
  field mission, 29
  finding allies, 42
  foreign aid matrix, 103
  formerly socialist nations, 13, 25
  future shifts, 92
  government agencies, 12*n*, 98
  merger with State Department, 41, 41*n*
  multilateral development bank policy,
    43
  Office of Foreign Disaster Assistance
    (OFDA), 24, 30, 92
  Office of Transition Initiatives, 22-23,
    92
  political role, 41-42
  reorganizing, 92, 93
  shift in programming processes, 29
  timeline for budgetary process, 36*t*
Uvin, Peter, 23*n*

vaccines, 76
Van de Walle, Nick, 79*n*
Venezuela, 64*n*
vice presidents, 44
Vietnam, 63
Vietnam War, 46
violence, 60-61
volatility, costs of, 78

Wallensteen, Peter, 58*n*
Wangwe, Sam, 65*n*
water issues, 66-69
  efficiency, 68
  International Conference on Water and the
    Environment, 68*n*
  shortages, 4
  waters, international, protection, 102
weapons of mass destruction, 81
West Bank/Gaza, aid levels, 29
Western Europe, prosperity, 63
Wharton, Clifton R., Jr., 27, 27*n*
Wharton Report, 27, 27*n*
White House
  as actor in politics of foreign aid, 44-45
  USAID programs, 42
women
  future policy, 85
  humane concerns, 20
Woodrow, Peter J., 25*n*
Working Group on Emerging and
    Re-emerging Infectious Diseases, 76*n*
World Bank 6*n*, 23*n*, 32*t*, 63*t*, 64*n*, 77*t*, 78*t*,
    82*n*
  described, 98
  economic policy reform, 31
  field mission, 29
  focus, 31
  food supply, 70
  funding amounts, 11*t*
  ozone depletion, 74
  Post-Conflict Unit, 23
  studies of, 2
  US arrears, 15
  water issues, 59, 68
World Food Program, 32*t*
World Food Program (WFP), 100-101
World Food Summit, 69*n*
World Health Organization (WHO), 12, 32*t*,
    76
  described, 101
  leadership, 91
World Resources Institute, 75*n*
World Trade Organization (WTO)
  agricultural commodities, 70
  Battle of Seattle, 79, 80
World Water Council, 69
Wye River Agreement, 15, 18

Yemen, 63
Yugoslavia, 59

Zaire, 24-25*n*

Other Publications from the Institute for International Economics

*= out of print

POLICY ANALYSES IN
INTERNATIONAL ECONOMICS Series

1 The Lending Policies of the International Monetary Fund* John Williamson
August 1982 ISBN 0-88132-000-5
2 "Reciprocity": A New Approach to World Trade Policy?* William R. Cline
September 1982 ISBN 0-88132-001-3
3 Trade Policy in the 1980s*
C. Fred Bergsten and William R. Cline
November 1982 ISBN 0-88132-002-1
4 International Debt and the Stability of the World Economy* William R. Cline
September 1983 ISBN 0-88132-010-2
5 The Exchange Rate System*, Second Edition
John Williamson
Sept. 1983, rev. June 1985 ISBN 0-88132-034-X
6 Economic Sanctions in Support of Foreign Policy Goals*
Gary Clyde Hufbauer and Jeffrey J. Schott
October 1983 ISBN 0-88132-014-5
7 A New SDR Allocation?* John Williamson
March 1984 ISBN 0-88132-028-5
8 An International Standard for Monetary Stabilization* Ronald L. McKinnon
March 1984 ISBN 0-88132-018-8
9 The YEN/Dollar Agreement: Liberalizing Japanese Capital Markets* Jeffrey A. Frankel
December 1984 ISBN 0-88132-035-8
10 Bank Lending to Developing Countries: The Policy Alternatives* C. Fred Bergsten, William R. Cline, and John Williamson
April 1985 ISBN 0-88132-032-3
11 Trading for Growth: The Next Round of Trade Negotiations*
Gary Clyde Hufbauer and Jeffrey R. Schott
September 1985 ISBN 0-88132-033-1
12 Financial Intermediation Beyond the Debt Crisis* Donald R. Lessard, John Williamson
September 1985 ISBN 0-88132-021-8
13 The United States-Japan Economic Problem*
C. Fred Bergsten and William R. Cline
October 1985, 2d ed. January 1987
ISBN 0-88132-060-9
14 Deficits and the Dollar: The World Economy at Risk* Stephen Marris
December 1985, 2d ed. November 1987
ISBN 0-88132-067-6
15 Trade Policy for Troubled Industries*
Gary Clyde Hufbauer and Howard R. Rosen
March 1986 ISBN 0-88132-020-X
16 The United States and Canada: The Quest for Free Trade* Paul Wonnacott, with an Appendix by John Williamson
March 1987 ISBN 0-88132-056-0
17 Adjusting to Success: Balance of Payments Policy in the East Asian NICs*
Bela Balassa and John Williamson
June 1987, rev. April 1990 ISBN 0-88132-101-X
18 Mobilizing Bank Lending to Debtor Countries* William R. Cline
June 1987 ISBN 0-88132-062-5
19 Auction Quotas and United States Trade Policy* C. Fred Bergsten, Kimberly Ann Elliott, Jeffrey J. Schott, and Wendy E. Takacs
September 1987 ISBN 0-88132-050-1
20 Agriculture and the GATT: Rewriting the Rules* Dale E. Hathaway
September 1987 ISBN 0-88132-052-8
21 Anti-Protection: Changing Forces in United States Trade Politics*
I. M. Destler and John S. Odell
September 1987 ISBN 0-88132-043-9
22 Targets and Indicators: A Blueprint for the International Coordination of Economic Policy* John Williamson and Marcus H. Miller
September 1987 ISBN 0-88132-051-X
23 Capital Flight: The Problem and Policy Responses* Donald R. Lessard and John Williamson
December 1987 ISBN 0-88132-059-5
24 United States-Canada Free Trade: An Evaluation of the Agreement*
Jeffrey J. Schott
April 1988 ISBN 0-88132-072-2
25 Voluntary Approaches to Debt Relief*
John Williamson
Sept.1988, rev. May 1989 ISBN 0-88132-098-6
26 American Trade Adjustment: The Global Impact* William R. Cline
March 1989 ISBN 0-88132-095-1
27 More Free Trade Areas?* Jeffrey J. Schott
May 1989 ISBN 0-88132-085-4
28 The Progress of Policy Reform in Latin America* John Williamson
January 1990 ISBN 0-88132-100-1
29 The Global Trade Negotiations: What Can Be Achieved?* Jeffrey J. Schott
September 1990 ISBN 0-88132-137-0
30 Economic Policy Coordination: Requiem or Prologue?* Wendy Dobson
April 1991 ISBN 0-88132-102-8

Toward Renewed Economic Growth in Latin America* Bela Balassa, Gerardo M. Bueno, Pedro-Pablo Kuczynski, and Mario Henrique Simonsen
1986 ISBN 0-88132-045-5

Capital Flight and Third World Debt*
Donald R. Lessard and John Williamson, editors
1987 ISBN 0-88132-053-6

The Canada-United States Free Trade Agreement: The Global Impact*
Jeffrey J. Schott and Murray G. Smith, editors
1988 ISBN 0-88132-073-0

World Agricultural Trade: Building a Consensus*
William M. Miner and Dale E. Hathaway, editors
1988 ISBN 0-88132-071-3

Japan in the World Economy*
Bela Balassa and Marcus Noland
1988 ISBN 0-88132-041-2

America in the World Economy: A Strategy for the 1990s C. Fred Bergsten
1988 ISBN 0-88132-089-7

Managing the Dollar: From the Plaza to the Louvre* Yoichi Funabashi
1988, 2d ed. 1989 ISBN 0-88132-097-8

United States External Adjustment and the World Economy* William R. Cline
May 1989 ISBN 0-88132-048-X

Free Trade Areas and U.S. Trade Policy*
Jeffrey J. Schott, editor
May 1989 ISBN 0-88132-094-3

Dollar Politics: Exchange Rate Policymaking in the United States*
I.M. Destler and C. Randall Henning
September 1989 ISBN 0-88132-079-X

Latin American Adjustment: How Much Has Happened?* John Williamson, editor
April 1990 ISBN 0-88132-125-7

The Future of World Trade in Textiles and Apparel* William R. Cline
1987, 2d ed. June 1990 ISBN 0-88132-110-9

Completing the Uruguay Round: A Results-Oriented Approach to the GATT Trade Negotiations* Jeffrey J. Schott, editor
September 1990 ISBN 0-88132-130-3

Economic Sanctions Reconsidered (2 volumes)
Economic Sanctions Reconsidered: Supplemental Case Histories
Gary Clyde Hufbauer, Jeffrey J. Schott, and Kimberly Ann Elliott
1985, 2d ed. Dec. 1990 ISBN cloth 0-88132-115-X
ISBN paper 0-88132-105-2

Economic Sanctions Reconsidered: History and Current Policy
Gary Clyde Hufbauer, Jeffrey J. Schott, and Kimberly Ann Elliott
December 1990 ISBN cloth 0-88132-140-0
ISBN paper 0-88132-136-2

Pacific Basin Developing Countries: Prospects for the Future* Marcus Noland
January 1991 ISBN cloth 0-88132-141-9
ISBN 0-88132-081-1

Currency Convertibility in Eastern Europe*
John Williamson, editor
October 1991 ISBN 0-88132-128-1

International Adjustment and Financing: The Lessons of 1985-1991* C. Fred Bergsten, editor
January 1992 ISBN 0-88132-112-5

North American Free Trade: Issues and Recommendations
Gary Clyde Hufbauer and Jeffrey J. Schott
April 1992 ISBN 0-88132-120-6

Narrowing the U.S. Current Account Deficit*
Allen J. Lenz
June 1992 ISBN 0-88132-103-6

The Economics of Global Warming
William R. Cline/*June 1992* ISBN 0-88132-132-X

U.S. Taxation of International Income: Blueprint for Reform* Gary Clyde Hufbauer, assisted by Joanna M. van Rooij
October 1992 ISBN 0-88132-134-6

Who's Bashing Whom? Trade Conflict in High-Technology Industries Laura D'Andrea Tyson
November 1992 ISBN 0-88132-106-0

Korea in the World Economy Il SaKong
January 1993 ISBN 0-88132-183-4

Pacific Dynamism and the International Economic System*
C. Fred Bergsten and Marcus Noland, editors
May 1993 ISBN 0-88132-196-6

Economic Consequences of Soviet Disintegration*
John Williamson, editor
May 1993 ISBN 0-88132-190-7

Reconcilable Differences? United States-Japan Economic Conflict
C. Fred Bergsten and Marcus Noland
June 1993 ISBN 0-88132-129-X

Does Foreign Exchange Intervention Work?
Kathryn M. Dominguez and Jeffrey A. Frankel
September 1993 ISBN 0-88132-104-4

Sizing Up U.S. Export Disincentives*
J. David Richardson
September 1993 ISBN 0-88132-107-9

NAFTA: An Assessment
Gary Clyde Hufbauer and Jeffrey J. Schott/*rev. ed.*
October 1993 ISBN 0-88132-199-0

Adjusting to Volatile Energy Prices
Philip K. Verleger, Jr.
November 1993 ISBN 0-88132-069-2

The Political Economy of Policy Reform
John Williamson, editor
January 1994 ISBN 0-88132-195-8

Measuring the Costs of Protection
in the United States
Gary Clyde Hufbauer and Kimberly Ann Elliott
January 1994   ISBN 0-88132-108-7
The Dynamics of Korean Economic Development
Cho Soon
March 1994   ISBN 0-88132-162-1
Reviving the European Union*
C. Randall Henning, Eduard Hochreiter, and Gary
Clyde Hufbauer, Editors
April 1994   ISBN 0-88132-208-3
China in the World Economy   Nicholas R. Lardy
April 1994   ISBN 0-88132-200-8
Greening the GATT: Trade, Environment, and the
Future   Daniel C. Esty
July 1994   ISBN 0-88132-205-9
Western Hemisphere Economic Integration
Gary Clyde Hufbauer and Jeffrey J. Schott
July 1994   ISBN 0-88132-159-1
Currencies and Politics in the United States,
Germany, and Japan
C. Randall Henning
September 1994   ISBN 0-88132-127-3
Estimating Equilibrium Exchange Rates
John Williamson, editor
September 1994   ISBN 0-88132-076-5
Managing the World Economy: Fifty Years After
Bretton Woods   Peter B. Kenen, editor
September 1994   ISBN 0-88132-212-1
Reciprocity and Retaliation in U.S. Trade Policy
Thomas O. Bayard and Kimberly Ann Elliott
September 1994   ISBN 0-88132-084-6
The Uruguay Round: An Assessment
Jeffrey J. Schott, assisted by Johanna W. Buurman
November 1994   ISBN 0-88132-206-7
Measuring the Costs of Protection in Japan
Yoko Sazanami, Shujiro Urata, and Hiroki Kawai
January 1995   ISBN 0-88132-211-3
Foreign Direct Investment in the United States,
3rd Ed.   Edward M. Graham and Paul R. Krugman
January 1995   ISBN 0-88132-204-0
The Political Economy of Korea-United States
Cooperation*
C. Fred Bergsten and Il SaKong, editors/*February
1995*   ISBN 0-88132-213-X
International Debt Reexamined   William R. Cline
February 1995   ISBN 0-88132-083-8
American Trade Politics, 3rd Ed.   I.M. Destler
April 1995   ISBN 0-88132-215-6
Managing Official Export Credits: The Quest for a
Global Regime*   John E. Ray
July 1995   ISBN 0-88132-207-5
Asia Pacific Fusion: Japan's Role in APEC*
Yoichi Funabashi
October 1995   ISBN 0-88132-224-5

Korea-United States Cooperation in the New
World Order*
C. Fred Bergsten and Il SaKong, editors
February 1996   ISBN 0-88132-226-1
Why Exports Really Matter! * ISBN 0-88132-221-0
Why Exports Matter More!* ISBN 0-88132-229-6
J. David Richardson and Karin Rindal
July 1995; February 1996
Global Corporations and National Governments
Edward M. Graham
May 1996   ISBN 0-88132-111-7
Global Economic Leadership and the Group of
Seven   C. Fred Bergsten and C. Randall Henning
May 1996   ISBN 0-88132-218-0
The Trading System After the Uruguay Round
John Whalley and Colleen Hamilton
July 1996   ISBN 0-88132-131-1
Private Capital Flows to Emerging Markets After
the Mexican Crisis   Guillermo A. Calvo,
Morris Goldstein, and Eduard Hochreiter
September 1996   ISBN 0-88132-232-6
The Crawling Band as an Exchange Rate Regime:
Lessons from Chile, Colombia, and Israel
John Williamson
September 1996   ISBN 0-88132-231-8
Flying High: Liberalizing Civil Aviation in the
Asia Pacific
Gary Clyde Hufbauer and Christopher Findlay
November 1996   ISBN 0-88132-227-X
Measuring the Costs of Visible Protection in
Korea   Namdoo Kim
November 1996   ISBN 0-88132-236-9
The World Trading System: Challenges Ahead
Jeffrey J. Schott
December 1996   ISBN 0-88132-235-0
Has Globalization Gone Too Far?   Dani Rodrik
March 1997   ISBN cloth 0-88132-243-1
Korea-United States Economic Relationship
C. Fred Bergsten and Il SaKong, editors
March 1997   ISBN 0-88132-240-7
Summitry in the Americas: A Progress Report
Richard E. Feinberg
April 1997   ISBN 0-88132-242-3
Corruption and the Global Economy
Kimberly Ann Elliott
June 1997   ISBN 0-88132-233-4
Regional Trading Blocs in the World Economic
System   Jeffrey A. Frankel
October 1997   ISBN 0-88132-202-4
Sustaining the Asia Pacific Miracle:
Environmental Protection and Economic
Integration   André Dua and Daniel C. Esty
October 1997   ISBN 0-88132-250-4
Trade and Income Distribution   William R. Cline
November 1997   ISBN 0-88132-216-4

Global Competition Policy
Edward M. Graham and J. David Richardson
December 1997   ISBN 0-88132-166-4
Unfinished Business: Telecommunications after
the Uruguay Round
Gary Clyde Hufbauer and Erika Wada
December 1997   ISBN 0-88132-257-1
Financial Services Liberalization in the WTO
Wendy Dobson and Pierre Jacquet
June 1998   ISBN 0-88132-254-7
Restoring Japan's Economic Growth
Adam S. Posen
September 1998   ISBN 0-88132-262-8
Measuring the Costs of Protection in China
Zhang Shuguang, Zhang Yansheng, and Wan
Zhongxin
November 1998   ISBN 0-88132-247-4
Foreign Direct Investment and Development: The
New Policy Agenda for Developing Countries
and Economies in Transition
Theodore H. Moran
December 1998   ISBN 0-88132-258-X
Behind the Open Door: Foreign Enterprises in the
Chinese Marketplace   Daniel H. Rosen
January 1999   ISBN 0-88132-263-6
Toward A New International Financial
Architecture: A Practical Post-Asia Agenda
Barry Eichengreen
February 1999   ISBN 0-88132-270-9
Is the U.S. Trade Deficit Sustainable?
Catherine L. Mann/*September 1999*
ISBN 0-88132-265-2
Safeguarding Prosperity in a Global Financial
System: The Future International Financial
Architecture, Independent Task Force Report
Sponsored by the Council on Foreign Relations
Morris Goldstein, Project Director
October 1999   ISBN 0-88132-287-3
Avoiding the Apocalypse: The Future of the Two
Koreas   Marcus Noland
June 2000   ISBN 0-88132-278-4
Assessing Financial Vulnerability: An Early
Warning System for Emerging Markets
Morris Goldstein, Graciela Kaminsky, and Carmen
Reinhart
June 2000   ISBN 0-88132-237-7
Global Electronic Commerce: A Policy Primer
Catherine L. Mann, Sue E. Eckert, and Sarah
Cleeland Knight
July 2000   ISBN 0-88132-274-1
The WTO after Seattle
Jeffrey J. Schott, editor
July 2000   ISBN 0-88132-290-3
Intellectual Property Rights in the Global
Economy   Keith E. Maskus
August 2000   ISBN 0-88132-282-2

The Political Economy of the Asian Financial
Crisis   Stephan Haggard
August 2000   ISBN 0-88132-283-0
Transforming Foreign Aid: United States
Assistance in the 21st Century   Carol Lancaster
August 2000   ISBN 0-88132-291-1

SPECIAL REPORTS

1   Promoting World Recovery: A Statement on
     Global Economic Strategy*
     by Twenty-six Economists from Fourteen
     Countries
     December 1982   ISBN 0-88132-013-7
2   Prospects for Adjustment in Argentina,
     Brazil, and Mexico: Responding to the Debt
     Crisis*   John Williamson, editor
     June 1983   ISBN 0-88132-016-1
3   Inflation and Indexation: Argentina, Brazil,
     and Israel*   John Williamson, editor
     March 1985   ISBN 0-88132-037-4
4   Global Economic Imbalances*
     C. Fred Bergsten, editor
     March 1986   ISBN 0-88132-042-0
5   African Debt and Financing*
     Carol Lancaster and John Williamson, editors
     May 1986   ISBN 0-88132-044-7
6   Resolving the Global Economic Crisis: After
     Wall Street*
     Thirty-three Economists from Thirteen
     Countries
     December 1987   ISBN 0-88132-070-6
7   World Economic Problems
     Kimberly Ann Elliott and John Williamson,
     editors
     April 1988   ISBN 0-88132-055-2
     Reforming World Agricultural Trade*
     Twenty-nine Professionals from Seventeen
     Countries
     1988   ISBN 0-88132-088-9
8   Economic Relations Between the United
     States and Korea: Conflict or Cooperation?*
     Thomas O. Bayard and Soo-Gil Young, editors
     January 1989   ISBN 0-88132-068-4
9   Whither APEC? The Progress to Date and
     Agenda for the Future
     C. Fred Bergsten, editor
     October 1997   ISBN 0-88132-248-2
10   Economic Integration of the Korean
     Peninsula   Marcus Noland, editor
     January 1998   ISBN 0-88132-255-5
11   Restarting Fast Track   Jeffrey J. Schott, editor
     April 1998   ISBN 0-88132-259-8
12   Launching New Global Trade Talks:
     An Action Agenda   Jeffrey J. Schott, editor
     September 1998   ISBN 0-88132-266-0

WORKS IN PROGRESS

The Impact of Increased Trade on
Organized Labor in the United States
Robert E. Baldwin
New Regional Arrangements and the World
Economy
C. Fred Bergsten
The Globalization Backlash in Europe and the
United States
C. Fred Bergsten, Pierre Jacquet, and Karl Kaiser
The U.S.-Japan Economic Relationship
C. Fred Bergsten, Marcus Noland, and
Takatoshi Ito
China's Entry to the World Economy
Richard N. Cooper
World Capital Markets: Challenges to
the G-10
Wendy Dobson and Gary Clyde Hufbauer
The ILO in the World Economy
Kimberly Ann Elliott
Reforming Economic Sanctions
Kimberly Ann Elliott, Gary C. Hufbauer, and
Jeffrey J. Schott
Free Trade in Labor Agency Services
Kimberly Ann Elliott and J. David Richardson
The *Chaebol* and Structural Problems in Korea
Edward M. Graham
Fighting the Wrong Enemy: Antiglobal Activists
and Multinational Enterprises
Edward M. Graham
Ex-Im Bank in the 21st Century
Gary Clyde Hufbauer and Rita Rodriquez, eds.
NAFTA: A Seven Year Appraisal of the Trade,
Environment, and Labor Agreements
Gary Clyde Hufbauer and Jeffrey J. Schott
Prospects for Western Hemisphere Free Trade
Gary Clyde Hufbauer and Jeffrey J. Schott

Price Integration in the World Economy
Gary Clyde Hufbauer, Erika Wada, and
Tony Warren
Reforming the IMF
Peter Kenen
Imports, Exports, and American Industrial
Workers since 1979
Lori G. Kletzer
Reemployment Experiences of Trade-
Displaced Americans
Lori G. Kletzer
Globalization and Creative Destruction in the
US Textile and Apparel Industry
James Levinsohn
Measuring the Costs of Protection in Europe
Patrick Messerlin
Dollarization, Currency Blocs, and U.S. Policy
Adams S. Posen
Germany in the World Economy after the
EMU
Adam S. Posen
Japan's Financial Crisis and Its Parallels to
U.S. Experience
Adam S. Posen and Ryoichi Mikitani, eds.
Sizing Up Globalization: The Globalization
Balance Sheet Capstone Volume
J. David Richardson
Why Global Integration Matters Most!
J. David Richardson and Howard Lewis
Worker Perceptions and Pressures in the
Global Economy
Matthew J. Slaughter
India in the World Economy
T. N. Srinivasan and Suresh D. Tendulka
Exchange-Rate Regimes for East Asia:
Reviving the Intermediate Option
John Williamson

Australia, New Zealand, and Papua New Guinea
D.A. INFORMATION SERVICES
648 Whitehorse Road
Mitcham, Victoria 3132, Australia
tel: 61-3-9210-7777
fax: 61-3-9210-7788
e-mail: service@dadirect.com.au
http://www.dadirect.com.au

Argentina
World Publications SA.
Av. Cordoba 1877
1120 Buenos Aires, Argentina
tel/fax: (54 11) 4815 8156
e-mail:
http://wpbooks@infovia.com.ar

Canada
RENOUF BOOKSTORE
5369 Canotek Road, Unit 1,
Ottawa, Ontario K1J 9J3, Canada
tel: 613-745-2665
fax: 613-745-7660
http://www.renoufbooks.com

Caribbean
SYSTEMATICS STUDIES LIMITED
St. Augustine Shopping Centre
Eastern Main Road, St. Augustine
Trinidad and Tobago, West Indies
tel: 868-645-8466
fax: 868-645-8467
e-mail: tobe@trinidad.net

People's Republic of China
(including Hong
Kong) **and Taiwan** (sales
representatives):
Tom Cassidy
Cassidy & Associates
70 Battery Place, Ste 220
New York, NY 10280
tel: 212-706-2200   fax: 212-706-2254
e-mail: CHINACAS@Prodigy.net

Colombia, Ecuador, and Peru
Infoenlace Ltda
Attn: Octavio Rojas
Calle 72 No. 13-23 Piso 3
Edificio Nueva Granada, Bogota, D.C.
Colombia
tel: (571) 255 8783 or 255 7969
fax: (571) 248 0808 or 217 6435

United Kingdom and Europe (including Russia and Turkey)
The Eurospan Group
3 Henrietta Street, Covent Garden
London WC2E 8LU England
tel: 44-20-7240-0856
fax: 44-20-7379-0609
http://www.eurospan.co.uk

India, Bangladesh, Nepal, and Sri Lanka
Viva Books Pvt.
Mr. Vinod Vasishtha
4325/3, Ansari Rd.
Daryaganj, New Delhi-110002
INDIA
tel: 91-11-327-9280
fax: 91-11-326-7224 ,
e-mail: vinod.viva@gndel.globalnet.
ems.vsnl.net.in

Japan and the Republic of Korea
United Publishers Services, Ltd.
Kenkyu-Sha Bldg.
9, Kanda Surugadai 2-Chome
Chiyoda-Ku, Tokyo 101
JAPAN
tel: 81-3-3291-4541;
fax: 81-3-3292-8610
e-mail: saito@ups.co.jp
**For trade accounts only.
Individuals will find IIE books in leading Tokyo bookstores.**

Northern Africa and the Middle East (Egypt, Algeria, Bahrain, Palestine, Jordan, Kuwait, Lebanon, Libya, Morocco, Oman, Qatar, Saudi Arabia, Syria, Tunisia, Yemen, and United Arab Emirates)
Middle East Readers Information Center (MERIC)
2 bahgat Aly Street
El-Masry Towers, Tower #D, Apt. #24, First Floor
Zamalek, Cairo EGYPT
tel: 202-341-3824/340 3818;
fax 202-341-9355
http://www.meric-co.com

South Africa
Pat Bennink
Dryad Books
PO Box 11684
Vorna Valley 1686
South Africa
tel: +27 14 576 1332
fax: +27 82 899 9156
e-mail: dryad@hixnet.co.za

South America
Julio E. Emod
Publishers Marketing & Research
Associates, c/o HARBRA
Rua Joaquim Tavora, 629
04015-001 Sao Paulo, Brasil
tel: (55) 11-571-1122;
fax: (55) 11-575-6876
e-mail: emod@harbra.com.br

Taiwan
Unifacmanu Trading Co., Ltd.
1F, No. 91, Ho-Ping East Rd, Sect. 1
Taipei 10609, Taiwan
tel: 886-2-23419646
fax: 886-2-23943103
e-mail: winjoin@ms12.hinet.net

Thailand
Asia Books 5 Sukhumvit Rd. Soi 61
Bangkok 10110 Thailand
(phone 662-714-0740-2 Ext: 221, 222, 223
fax: (662) 391-2277)
e-mail: purchase@asiabooks.co.th
http://www.asiabooksonline.com

**Visit our Web site at:
http://www.iie.com
E-mail orders to:
orders@iie.com**